THE CITY B|

THE ULTIMATE ORLANDO ITINERARY

ORLANDO

TRAVEL GUIDE

DIANA L.
MITCHELL

Dear reader, thanks a lot for purchasing my book.

To help you plan your trip even more efficiently, I have included an interactive map powered by Google My Maps.

To access it, scan the QR code below.

Happy travelling!

A Note to Our Valued Readers

Thank you for choosing this travel guide as your companion for exploring the world.

I want to take a moment to address a concern you might have regarding the absence of photographs in this book.

As an independent author and publisher, I strive to deliver high-quality, informative content at an affordable price.

Including photographs in a printed book, however, presents significant challenges. Licensing high-quality images can be extremely costly, and unfortunately, I have no control over the print quality of images within the book.

Because these guides are printed and shipped by Amazon, I am unable to review the final print quality before they reach your hands.

So, rather than risk compromising your reading experience with subpar visuals, I've chosen to focus on providing detailed, insightful content that will help you make the most of your travels.

While this guide may not contain photos, it's packed with valuable information, insider tips, and recommendations to ensure you have an enriching and memorable journey.

Additionally, there's an interactive map powered by Google My Maps—an essential tool to help you plan your trip.

I encourage you to supplement your reading with online resources where you can find up-to-date images and visuals of the destinations covered in this guide.

I hope you find this book a helpful and inspiring resource as you embark on your next adventure.

Thank you for your understanding and support.

Safe travels,

Diana

Table of Contents

Welcome to Orlando

Welcome to Orlando, a vibrant city known as the "Theme Park Capital of the World." Bursting with excitement and entertainment, Orlando is a hub of family-friendly attractions, world-class resorts, and outdoor adventures, making it one of the most popular travel destinations in the United States. Whether you're a first-time visitor or a seasoned traveler, the city's iconic attractions, diverse neighborhoods, and sunny weather offer endless opportunities for fun and relaxation.

Orlando is composed of a variety of neighborhoods, each with its unique character and charm. From the bustling International Drive with its array of attractions and restaurants to the historic districts of Downtown Orlando and Winter Park, there's something for everyone. The city's surrounding areas, like Kissimmee and Lake Buena Vista, also offer a rich tapestry of experiences and accommodations.

The city is home to some of the world's most famous theme parks, such as Walt Disney World Resort, Universal Orlando Resort, and SeaWorld Orlando. It's a global hub for entertainment and hospitality, featuring spectacular shows, thrilling rides, and immersive experiences. Whether you're exploring the magic of Disney, the wizarding world of Harry Potter, enjoying a round of golf, or savoring culinary delights from around the globe, Orlando promises an unforgettable experience.

Join us as we guide you through the best of what Orlando has to offer, providing tips and insights to help you make the most of your visit to this extraordinary city.

Why visit Orlando?

Orlando, often dubbed "The City Beautiful," is a vibrant destination that offers a unique blend of entertainment, nature, and culture, attracting millions of visitors each year. Here are some compelling reasons why Orlando should be on your travel radar:

World-Famous Theme Parks

Orlando is the theme park capital of the world, home to iconic attractions like Walt Disney World Resort, Universal Orlando Resort, and SeaWorld Orlando. Whether you're looking to explore the magical kingdoms of Disney, experience the thrilling rides at Universal's Islands of Adventure, or enjoy marine life at SeaWorld, these parks offer endless fun for all ages.

Cultural Diversity

Orlando boasts a rich cultural tapestry, with a diverse population that influences its neighborhoods, festivals, and food scene. From the vibrant Caribbean flavors in Little Haiti to the cultural events celebrating Latin heritage, Orlando offers a multicultural experience that enriches your visit.

Outdoor Adventures and Nature

Beyond the theme parks, Orlando offers numerous opportunities to connect with nature. Explore the lush landscapes of the Everglades on an airboat tour, paddle through the tranquil waters of the Wekiva River, or visit the Harry P. Leu Gardens for a peaceful retreat amidst beautiful flora. Orlando's natural beauty provides a serene contrast to its bustling attractions.

Shopping Paradise

Orlando is a shopper's dream, with an array of options from luxury malls like The Mall at Millenia and Orlando International Premium Outlets to quirky boutiques in Winter Park. Whether you're hunting for high-end fashion, unique souvenirs, or the latest gadgets, Orlando has something for every shopper.

World-Class Museums and Art

Art and history enthusiasts will find plenty to explore in Orlando. The Orlando Museum of Art, the Charles Hosmer Morse Museum of American Art, and the Dr. Phillips Center for the Performing Arts offer a range of experiences from contemporary art to historical exhibitions and live performances.

Culinary Delights

Orlando's dining scene is as diverse as its population. Savor everything from international cuisines in the Mills 50 District to fresh seafood in Winter Park. Don't miss the chance to enjoy a farm-to-table meal at one of the city's many acclaimed restaurants, or indulge in the local favorite, Key lime pie.

Vibrant Nightlife and Entertainment

When the sun sets, Orlando comes alive with a variety of entertainment options. From the bustling nightlife of downtown Orlando to the lively atmosphere of Disney Springs and Universal CityWalk, there's something for everyone. Enjoy live music, comedy shows, or simply unwind at one of the many rooftop bars.

Historical Significance

Orlando offers a glimpse into Florida's rich history. Visit the Orange County Regional History Center to learn about the city's past, or take a trip to nearby historic sites like the Kennedy Space Center, where you can explore the history of space exploration and even meet an astronaut.

Beautiful Weather Year-Round

Orlando's warm climate makes it a perfect destination at any time of year. Whether you're visiting in the sunny summer months or the mild winter season, you can enjoy outdoor activities, festivals, and events year-round.

Charming Neighborhoods

Each neighborhood in Orlando has its own unique vibe. Stroll through the artsy streets of Thornton Park, explore the upscale shopping and dining in Winter Park, or enjoy the family-friendly atmosphere of Lake Nona. Every visit offers the opportunity to discover a new side of the city.

Orlando's blend of thrilling attractions, cultural richness, and natural beauty makes it a top destination for travelers. Whether you're here for the adventure of the theme parks, the tranquility of the outdoors, or the excitement of the nightlife, Orlando promises an unforgettable experience for everyone.

Getting Around

Public Transportation

Orlando offers a variety of public transportation options, making it accessible and convenient to navigate the city and surrounding areas without a car. Here's an overview of the key public transportation options, including the Lynx bus system and the SunRail commuter train.

Lynx Bus System

Overview:
- The Lynx bus system is the primary public transit service in Orlando and the Central Florida region, operated by the Central Florida Regional Transportation Authority.
- It serves Orange, Seminole, and Osceola counties, providing an extensive network of routes that connect key areas and attractions.

Bus Routes:
- **Local Buses:** These buses serve the city of Orlando and surrounding communities, making frequent stops along designated routes.
- **Express Buses:** Provide faster service with limited stops, mainly catering to commuters traveling between suburban areas and downtown Orlando.
- **FastLink Buses:** A specialized service offering limited-stop routes that focus on connecting major destinations like the Orlando International Airport, Downtown Orlando, and theme parks.

Using the Bus:
- **Fares:** Payment can be made using cash, a Lynx PawPass, or through the Lynx mobile app. Various fare options are available, including single rides, day passes, and multi-day passes.

- **Bus Stops:** Look for distinctive Lynx bus stop signs, which display route numbers and schedules. Real-time updates and route planning are available through the Lynx app or website.
- **Boarding:** Enter through the front door and pay the fare. Remember to signal your stop request by pulling the cord or pressing the stop button.

Popular Routes:
- **Link 50:** Connects downtown Orlando to the University of Central Florida (UCF) and Waterford Lakes, popular for students and residents.
- **Link 42:** Travels from the Orlando International Airport to Downtown Orlando, a key route for travelers.
- **Link 38:** Serves the tourist corridor along International Drive, providing access to theme parks and resorts.

SunRail Commuter Train

Overview:
- SunRail is a commuter rail service that runs through the Greater Orlando area, offering an alternative to road travel.
- The service is designed primarily for weekday commuters, connecting key locations from DeBary in the north to Poinciana in the south.

Route and Schedule:
- The SunRail line has multiple stations, including stops in Winter Park, Downtown Orlando, and Kissimmee.
- Trains operate during morning and evening peak hours, with reduced service during mid-day and late-night hours. Check the SunRail website for the latest schedule.

Using SunRail:
- **Fares:** Tickets can be purchased at stations via vending machines or through the SunRail mobile app. Various fare options are available, including one-way, round-trip, and monthly passes.
- **Stations:** Each station provides parking facilities, making it convenient for commuters to park and ride. Stations are equipped with amenities such as ticket machines, seating, and information boards.

I-Ride Trolley

Overview:
- The I-Ride Trolley is a popular transportation option for tourists, providing service along International Drive, a major entertainment and shopping district in Orlando.
- It offers a fun and affordable way to travel between attractions, hotels, and restaurants in the area.

Routes:
- **Red Line:** Runs along International Drive from Orlando Premium Outlets to SeaWorld Orlando and beyond.
- **Green Line:** Extends service to Universal Boulevard and connects to Universal Studios Orlando.

Using the I-Ride Trolley:
- **Fares:** Payment can be made on board with cash or by purchasing passes online or at various locations along the route. Options include single rides and multi-day passes.
- **Stops:** The trolley makes frequent stops along its routes, with clear signage indicating stop locations.

Experience:
- The I-Ride Trolley offers an easy and scenic way to explore one of Orlando's most vibrant areas, with access to shopping, dining, and entertainment.
- Orlando's public transportation system, including Lynx buses, SunRail, and the I-Ride Trolley, provides convenient and cost-effective ways to explore the city and its attractions. Whether you're commuting for work, heading to a theme park, or exploring local neighborhoods, you'll find a range of options to suit your travel needs.

Taxis and Rideshares

Orlando offers a variety of taxi and rideshare options that provide convenient and flexible transportation throughout the city and its surrounding areas. Here's a detailed look at local taxis, Uber, and Lyft, including how to use them, fare information, and tips for a smooth ride.

Local Taxis

Overview:
Orlando has several taxi companies, with taxis commonly found at airports, major hotels, and popular attractions. These taxis provide reliable service throughout the city.

How to Hail a Taxi:
- **Street Hailing:** While less common than in NYC, you can hail a taxi on the street in busy areas or at taxi stands near major attractions and hotels.
- **Taxi Stands:** Located at the Orlando International Airport, major hotels, and popular tourist destinations like theme parks.
- **Telephone Dispatch:** Many taxi companies offer phone dispatch services, making it easy to call for a ride.

Fare Information:
- **Base Fare:** Typically starts at around $2.50, with additional charges based on distance and time.
- **Surcharges:** Additional charges may apply during peak hours, holidays, or for extra passengers and luggage.
- **Tolls:** Any tolls encountered during the trip are added to the fare.
- **Tips:** A customary tip for taxi drivers is 15-20% of the total fare.
- **Payment:** Accepted in cash and credit/debit cards. Ensure the taxi is equipped with a card reader if you plan to pay by card.

Tips for a Smooth Ride:
- **Provide Clear Directions:** Have your destination address ready and communicate it clearly to the driver.
- **Safety:** Note the taxi's company name and driver's ID, typically displayed on the dashboard.
- **Receipt:** Always ask for a receipt at the end of your ride for record-keeping or in case you need to retrieve lost items.

Overview:

- Uber and Lyft are popular rideshare services in Orlando, offering convenient, app-based transportation options.
- These services provide a range of vehicle types, from budget-friendly rides to luxury options.

Using Uber and Lyft:

- **Download the App:** Available on both iOS and Android platforms.
- **Create an Account:** Sign up with your email, phone number, and payment information.
- **Request a Ride:** Enter your destination and choose the type of ride (e.g., UberX, UberPOOL, Lyft, Lyft XL).
- **Track Your Ride:** The app provides real-time tracking of your driver's location and estimated arrival time.
- **Payment:** Automatically charged to your registered payment method. Tips can be added through the app.

Fare Information:

- **Base Fare:** Varies by service type and time of day.
- **Surge Pricing:** During peak times or high demand, prices may increase due to surge pricing.
- **Tolls:** Any applicable tolls are added to the fare.
- **Tips:** Tipping is optional but appreciated and can be done through the app.

Service Options:

- **UberX/Lyft:** Standard ride for up to four passengers.
- **UberPOOL/Lyft Shared:** Shared rides with other passengers heading in the same direction, offering a lower fare.
- **UberXL/Lyft XL:** Larger vehicles for groups up to six passengers.
- **Uber Black/Lyft Lux:** Premium black car service for a more luxurious ride experience.

Tips for a Smooth Ride:

- **Confirm Your Ride:** Verify the driver's name, vehicle make, model, and license plate before getting in.

- **Safety Features:** Both apps offer safety features such as sharing your trip status with friends and family and in-app emergency assistance.
- **Pickup Locations:** Choose a safe and convenient pickup location, especially in busy areas.
- **Ratings:** Rate your driver after the ride to provide feedback on your experience.

Comparisons and Considerations
- **Availability:** Taxis can be found at key locations like the airport and major hotels, while rideshare services are widely available and can be more convenient, especially for off-peak times or less busy areas.
- **Cost:** Rideshare fares can fluctuate due to surge pricing, whereas taxi fares are more consistent but may include surcharges during peak times.
- **Convenience:** Rideshare apps offer the convenience of cashless payment and real-time tracking, while taxis can be easily hailed at designated stands or called via dispatch services.

Whether you opt for a traditional taxi or a modern rideshare service like Uber or Lyft, Orlando provides a range of transportation options to suit your needs. Understanding how to use these services can help you navigate the city efficiently and enjoy your stay in Orlando.

Biking

Orlando Bike Share Program

Overview:
- Orlando's bike-sharing program offers a convenient and eco-friendly way to explore the city. It's part of the city's efforts to promote sustainable transportation and healthy living.
- The program features numerous bikes and docking stations throughout key areas, making it easy for both residents and visitors to access and use.

How the Bike Share Program Works:

- Membership Options: The program provides various membership plans to suit different needs:
- Single Ride: Ideal for occasional users, this option allows for a 30-minute ride at a fixed fee.
- Day Pass: Perfect for tourists, offering unlimited 30-minute rides within a 24-hour period.
- Monthly or Annual Membership: Best for residents, these memberships offer unlimited rides of a specified duration per day, often with the option for longer rides at an additional charge.
- Finding a Bike: Use the program's app or website to locate nearby docking stations and check bike availability.
- Unlocking a Bike: Bikes can be unlocked using the app, a membership key (for subscribers), or a ride code provided at the docking station.
- Riding and Returning: Enjoy your ride and return the bike to any docking station. Ensure the bike is securely docked to end your rental period.

Benefits of Using the Bike Share Program:

- Flexibility: Bikes provide an easy way to navigate through traffic and access areas not well-served by other forms of public transportation.
- Health and Fitness: Biking offers a great way to get some exercise while commuting or sightseeing.
- Environmentally Friendly: Using bikes reduces your carbon footprint, making it a greener alternative to driving or taking a taxi.

Tips for a Smooth Ride:

- Plan Your Route: Utilize the bike share app to plan safe and efficient routes, taking advantage of bike lanes and trails.
- Follow Traffic Rules: Always obey traffic signals and signs, use bike lanes where available, and signal your turns clearly.
- Safety Gear: Wearing a helmet is strongly recommended, along with reflective clothing or lights, especially for night riding.
- Station Availability: Check the app for docking station availability near your destination to avoid any last-minute inconveniences.

Popular Routes and Destinations:

- Lake Eola Park: Enjoy a leisurely ride around this scenic downtown lake, known for its swan boats and picturesque surroundings.

- Orlando Urban Trail: A multi-use trail that connects downtown Orlando to surrounding neighborhoods, offering a safe and pleasant biking experience.
- Cady Way Trail: Stretching from Orlando to the neighboring city of Winter Park, this trail is perfect for longer rides and connects to several parks and attractions.

Orlando's bike-sharing program provides an excellent way to explore the city, whether you're commuting to work, sightseeing, or just enjoying a leisurely ride. With a variety of membership options and numerous scenic routes, biking is a fun, healthy, and sustainable way to get around Orlando.

What to See and Do

Theme Parks and Attractions

Walt Disney World Resort

Walt Disney World Resort, located in Lake Buena Vista near Orlando, Florida, is the most visited vacation resort in the world. Covering nearly 25,000 acres, this magical destination offers four distinct theme parks: Magic Kingdom, Epcot, Disney's Hollywood Studios, and Disney's Animal Kingdom. Magic Kingdom, the crown jewel of the resort, is famous for its iconic Cinderella Castle and classic attractions like Space Mountain and Pirates of the Caribbean. Epcot is known for its celebration of human achievement and international cultures, featuring pavilions from around the globe and the futuristic World Showcase.

Disney's Hollywood Studios transports guests into the worlds of movies and television, offering thrilling rides like Star Wars: Rise of the Resistance and the Toy Story-themed Slinky Dog Dash. Disney's Animal Kingdom is a unique combination of a theme park and a zoo, home to the thrilling Expedition Everest roller coaster and the immersive Pandora – The World of Avatar. In addition to the theme parks, Walt Disney World Resort includes two water parks, Disney's Blizzard Beach and Disney's Typhoon Lagoon, as well as a wide array of hotels, dining, and shopping options.

The resort is renowned for its attention to detail, world-class customer service, and the ability to create unforgettable experiences for guests of all ages. Whether meeting beloved Disney characters, enjoying spectacular parades and fireworks, or indulging in exquisite cuisine, Walt Disney World offers a magical experience that continues to enchant millions of visitors each year.

Universal Orlando Resort

Universal Orlando Resort, situated in Orlando, Florida, is a premier vacation destination renowned for its thrilling attractions and immersive experiences. The resort encompasses three main parks: Universal Studios Florida, Universal's Islands of Adventure, and the water theme park, Universal's Volcano Bay. Universal Studios Florida is a dynamic theme park that brings movies and television to life, offering attractions like The Wizarding World of Harry Potter - Diagon Alley, where visitors can explore the magical world of Harry Potter and enjoy the thrilling Harry Potter and the Escape from Gringotts ride.

Universal's Islands of Adventure is home to some of the most exciting rides and attractions, including The Wizarding World of Harry Potter - Hogsmeade, featuring the iconic Hogwarts Castle and the thrilling ride Harry Potter and the Forbidden Journey. Other popular attractions include the Incredible Hulk Coaster and Jurassic Park River Adventure. Universal's Volcano Bay is a state-of-the-art water park themed around a lush, tropical island, offering a variety of slides, wave pools, and the innovative Krakatau Aqua Coaster.

In addition to the parks, Universal Orlando Resort offers the Universal CityWalk entertainment complex, featuring an array of dining, shopping, and nightlife options. The resort is known for its innovative use of technology, high-energy shows, and attractions that cater to thrill-seekers and families alike. With its unique blend of excitement and adventure, Universal Orlando Resort continues to be a top destination for visitors seeking an unforgettable vacation experience.

SeaWorld Orlando

SeaWorld Orlando is a renowned marine zoological park located in Orlando, Florida, offering a unique blend of thrilling rides, animal encounters, and educational exhibits. The park is part of the larger SeaWorld Parks & Entertainment chain and is known for its commitment to marine conservation and animal rescue efforts. One of the highlights of SeaWorld Orlando is its exciting roller coasters, including Mako, the tallest, fastest, and longest coaster in Orlando, and Manta, a flying coaster that mimics the graceful movements of a manta ray.

SeaWorld is also home to a variety of marine animals, including dolphins, sea lions, sharks, and the iconic orcas. The park's shows, such as the awe-inspiring Orca Encounter and the playful Dolphin Days, showcase the incredible abilities of these animals while promoting awareness of marine conservation. SeaWorld's newest attraction, Infinity Falls, offers guests an exhilarating raft ride through a lush jungle setting, culminating in a record-breaking drop.

14

Beyond the thrills, SeaWorld Orlando is dedicated to education and conservation, offering interactive exhibits like TurtleTrek and the Shark Encounter, where guests can learn about the importance of protecting marine life and habitats. The park also offers seasonal events such as SeaWorld's Christmas Celebration and the Electric Ocean summer festival, providing unique entertainment and festive experiences. With its combination of exciting attractions, animal encounters, and educational opportunities, SeaWorld Orlando offers a memorable and enriching experience for visitors of all ages.

ICON Park

ICON Park is a premier entertainment complex located in the heart of Orlando, Florida, offering a diverse array of attractions, dining, and shopping experiences. Spread over 20 acres on International Drive, ICON Park is known for its vibrant atmosphere and iconic attractions, making it a popular destination for both locals and tourists. The centerpiece of ICON Park is The Wheel, a towering observation wheel that provides breathtaking views of the Orlando skyline.

In addition to The Wheel, ICON Park features attractions such as Madame Tussauds Orlando, where visitors can interact with lifelike wax figures of celebrities and historical figures, and SEA LIFE Orlando Aquarium, which offers immersive underwater experiences showcasing a variety of marine life. The complex also hosts the Museum of Illusions, where guests can explore mind-bending exhibits and optical illusions.

ICON Park is not just about attractions; it is also a culinary hotspot with a wide range of dining options. From gourmet restaurants to casual eateries, visitors can enjoy a variety of cuisines, including seafood, Italian, and American classics. The Yard House, Tapa Toro, and Uncle Julio's are among the popular dining spots. Additionally, ICON Park features numerous shops and boutiques, perfect for souvenir shopping or finding unique gifts. The complex often hosts live entertainment, events, and seasonal celebrations, enhancing its appeal as a year-round destination. With its mix of thrilling attractions, delicious food, and vibrant nightlife, ICON Park offers a complete entertainment experience for visitors of all ages.

The Orlando Eye

The Orlando Eye, is one of the most recognizable landmarks in Orlando, Florida. Standing at 400 feet tall, The Orlando Eye is an observation wheel that offers panoramic views of the city and its surrounding areas. The structure features 30 climate-controlled capsules, each capable of holding up to 15 passengers, providing a comfortable and spacious environment for enjoying the stunning vistas. During the 20-minute ride, visitors can see iconic landmarks such as Walt Disney World, Universal Orlando Resort, and on clear days, even the Kennedy Space Center.

The Wheel's capsules are equipped with interactive tablets that provide information about the various points of interest visible from the top. The experience is further enhanced with LED lighting, which illuminates The Wheel in vibrant colors, making it a stunning spectacle, especially at night. The lighting system can be programmed to display a wide range of colors and patterns, often synchronized with special events and holidays, adding to its visual appeal. The Wheel at ICON Park is more than just an observation wheel; it offers a unique perspective of Orlando, allowing visitors to appreciate the city's landscape from a different angle. Whether it's a family outing, a romantic date night, or a fun adventure with friends, The Wheel provides a memorable experience that combines breathtaking views with modern technology and design. As part of the larger ICON Park complex, The Wheel is complemented by a variety of attractions, dining options, and entertainment, making it a must-visit destination for anyone exploring Orlando.

Fun Spot America

Fun Spot America is a popular family-owned amusement park with locations in Orlando and Kissimmee, Florida. Known for its classic American amusement park atmosphere, Fun Spot America offers a mix of thrilling rides, go-kart tracks, and arcade games that appeal to all ages. The park's most famous attractions include the "White Lightning" in Orlando, a wooden roller coaster that provides an exhilarating ride with plenty of airtime, and the "Freedom Flyer," a suspended steel coaster that offers smooth twists and turns.

Fun Spot America is also known for its expansive go-kart tracks, which are among the largest in the country. Visitors can choose from multiple tracks, each offering a unique racing experience. Additionally, the park offers a variety of rides suitable for younger children, making it a great destination for families.

Unlike many large theme parks, Fun Spot America does not charge an admission fee, allowing guests to pay per ride or purchase an all-day wristband. This flexible pricing model makes it an attractive option for those looking for a more affordable theme park experience. With its vibrant atmosphere, exciting attractions, and family-friendly environment, Fun Spot America continues to be a beloved destination for both locals and tourists in Central Florida.

LEGOLAND Florida Resort

LEGOLAND Florida Resort is a premier family destination located in Winter Haven, Florida, designed specifically for children aged 2 to 12. The resort includes a theme park, water park, and multiple on-site accommodations, all centered around the beloved LEGO brand. The theme park features more than 50 rides, shows, and attractions, many of which are interactive and educational.

Among the most popular attractions are the "LEGO NINJAGO The Ride," where guests can engage in a 4D interactive experience using hand gestures to defeat villains, and "Miniland USA," a stunning display of miniature cities built entirely out of LEGO bricks. The park is divided into various themed areas, each offering a different adventure, from the medieval "LEGO Kingdoms" to the prehistoric "LEGO Dino Island."

The adjacent LEGOLAND Water Park offers a variety of water-based attractions, including wave pools, lazy rivers, and water slides, all designed with a LEGO twist. The resort also features several themed hotels, such as the LEGOLAND Hotel and the LEGOLAND Pirate Island Hotel, which offer immersive experiences with LEGO-themed rooms and kid-friendly amenities. LEGOLAND Florida Resort is a place where creativity and imagination come to life, making it an ideal destination for families seeking a fun and engaging vacation.

The Holy Land Experience

The Holy Land Experience is a unique Christian theme park in Orlando, Florida, offering visitors an immersive journey through biblical history.

Designed to bring the Bible to life, this park features life-sized replicas of significant biblical sites, such as the Garden Tomb, the Great Temple, and the Wilderness Tabernacle. The park's centerpiece is the impressive re-creation of the ancient city of Jerusalem, complete with bustling marketplaces and historical architecture.

Visitors can witness live theatrical productions that depict various stories from the Bible, including the crucifixion and resurrection of Jesus Christ. These performances are not only educational but also deeply moving, providing a spiritual experience for many guests. In addition to the live shows, the Holy Land Experience offers various exhibits showcasing rare biblical artifacts, manuscripts, and artworks, giving visitors a deeper understanding of the history and context of the Christian faith.

The park also features beautifully landscaped gardens and serene prayer areas where visitors can reflect and meditate. Although the Holy Land Experience primarily caters to those interested in Christian history and teachings, its detailed recreations and performances can be appreciated by people of all faiths. The park's combination of entertainment, education, and spiritual enrichment makes it a distinctive attraction in Orlando's diverse landscape of theme parks and tourist destinations.

Crayola Experience Orlando

Crayola Experience Orlando is an interactive, family-friendly attraction located at The Florida Mall. This vibrant destination offers a colorful world of creativity, designed to engage the imaginations of children and adults alike. The Crayola Experience features over 25 hands-on attractions, allowing visitors to immerse themselves in the creative process. One of the highlights is the "Wrap It Up!" station, where guests can personalize and wrap their own Crayola crayon. Another popular activity is the "Melt & Mold," where crayons are melted down and molded into various shapes, such as rings or cars, creating unique keepsakes.

The attraction also includes the "Color Playground," a multi-level play area where kids can climb, slide, and explore, all while surrounded by vibrant Crayola-themed decor. The "Art Alive!" station allows visitors to bring their drawings to life by projecting them onto a large screen, where they can interact with other digital creations. For those interested in digital art, the "Be a Star" station lets visitors create personalized coloring pages by taking photos and transforming them into coloring book-style images.

In addition to the numerous activities, the Crayola Experience offers live demonstrations on how Crayola crayons are made, providing an educational aspect to the fun. The attraction also features a retail store filled with exclusive Crayola products, perfect for taking a piece of the experience home. With its focus on creativity, imagination, and hands-on fun, Crayola Experience Orlando is a must-visit destination for families looking to spend a colorful day together.

Ripley's Believe It or Not! Orlando

Ripley's Believe It or Not! Orlando is a fascinating attraction located on International Drive, known for its collection of oddities, curiosities, and unbelievable artifacts from around the world. Housed in a unique building that appears to be sinking into the ground, this "Odditorium" offers visitors a chance to explore the strange and the unusual through a series of themed galleries and exhibits. The museum features over 600 exhibits, each showcasing bizarre facts, incredible feats, and strange objects that challenge the imagination.

One of the most popular exhibits is the "Shrunken Heads," a display of real shrunken human heads from the Amazon. The museum also features a "Ripley's Wax Zone," where visitors can create their own wax hands as a memorable souvenir. Another crowd favorite is the "Space Oddities" exhibit, which includes rare artifacts related to space exploration, such as moon rocks and astronaut suits.

The "Odditorium" is also home to a variety of interactive displays, including optical illusions, mind-bending puzzles, and hands-on activities that make the experience engaging for all ages. The "Ripley's LaseRace" is an interactive laser maze where visitors can test their agility by navigating through a web of laser beams.

With its eclectic mix of the strange, the bizarre, and the just plain weird, Ripley's Believe It or Not! Orlando provides a fun and educational experience that leaves visitors amazed and entertained. It's an ideal stop for those looking to explore the oddities of the world in a fun, interactive environment.

WonderWorks Orlando

WonderWorks Orlando is an interactive, science-focused amusement park located on International Drive. Recognizable by its iconic upside-down building exterior, WonderWorks is designed to ignite the imagination and curiosity of visitors through a blend of education and entertainment. The attraction is divided into six themed zones, each offering unique, hands-on exhibits that challenge the mind and spark creativity.

The "Wonder Zones" include areas like the "Physical Challenge Zone," where guests can test their strength and endurance in activities such as lying on a bed of nails or experiencing a simulated earthquake. The "Space Discovery Zone" allows visitors to explore the mysteries of space through exhibits like the astronaut training gyroscope, which simulates the feeling of weightlessness.

One of the most popular attractions is the "Imagination Lab," where creativity takes center stage. Here, visitors can design and create digital art, play giant versions of classic board games, and explore the world of virtual reality. The "Light and Sound Zone" features exhibits that demonstrate the science behind light and sound, including a giant piano keyboard that plays music as you step on it.

WonderWorks also offers a thrilling indoor ropes course, the "Glow-In-The-Dark Ropes Course," where visitors can navigate a series of challenging obstacles suspended high above the ground. Additionally, the "4D XD Motion Theater" provides an immersive experience with 3D films enhanced by moving seats and special effects.

With its blend of education, creativity, and interactive fun, WonderWorks Orlando is a perfect destination for families, school groups, and anyone interested in exploring the wonders of science in an entertaining and engaging way.

Titanic: The Artifact Exhibition

Titanic: The Artifact Exhibition in Orlando offers visitors a poignant and immersive journey into the history of the ill-fated RMS Titanic. Located on International Drive, this museum features over 300 artifacts recovered from the Titanic's wreck site, as well as full-scale recreations of some of the ship's most famous rooms, including the Grand Staircase, the First-Class Parlor Suite, and the Promenade Deck.

The exhibition is designed to take visitors back in time to April 1912, providing an intimate look at the lives of the passengers and crew aboard the Titanic. Upon entering, guests receive a boarding pass with the name of an actual passenger, adding a personal connection as they explore the exhibits. Throughout the exhibition, visitors can learn about the ship's construction, the opulent lifestyle of its wealthiest passengers, and the tragic events that unfolded on the night of April 14, 1912.

One of the most moving aspects of the exhibition is the "Memorial Gallery," where visitors can discover the fate of the person whose boarding pass they received. The gallery honors the memory of those who perished in the disaster and celebrates the courage of the survivors.

The museum also features interactive displays, such as a simulated iceberg that allows visitors to feel the icy conditions the Titanic faced. Guided tours led by knowledgeable staff in period costumes add an extra layer of authenticity to the experience. Titanic: The Artifact Exhibition provides a respectful and educational exploration of one of history's most famous maritime tragedies, offering visitors a deep and emotional understanding of the Titanic's story.

Madame Tussauds Orlando

Madame Tussauds Orlando, located at ICON Park on International Drive, is a renowned wax museum that offers visitors the opportunity to get up close and personal with incredibly lifelike wax figures of their favorite celebrities, historical figures, and pop culture icons. The museum is part of the global Madame Tussauds brand, known for its meticulous attention to detail and craftsmanship in creating these stunning replicas.

Visitors to Madame Tussauds Orlando can explore a variety of themed galleries, each dedicated to different genres and eras. The "A-List Party" room features Hollywood stars such as Brad Pitt, Angelina Jolie, and Johnny Depp, allowing guests to mingle with the stars in a glamorous setting. In the "Music Zone," visitors can stand alongside music legends like Elvis Presley, Michael Jackson, and Taylor Swift, or even take the stage with them for a memorable photo opportunity.

The museum also celebrates American history and culture with its "History and Leaders" section, where figures like Abraham Lincoln, Martin Luther King Jr., and Albert Einstein are prominently displayed. For fans of superheroes, the "Justice League: A Call for Heroes" exhibit is a must-see, featuring lifelike figures of Batman, Superman, Wonder Woman, and other beloved characters in dynamic action poses.

Interactive elements throughout the museum enhance the experience, allowing visitors to pose, touch, and even interact with the wax figures. Whether taking a selfie with a Hollywood star or shaking hands with a world leader, Madame Tussauds Orlando offers a fun and engaging experience that brings visitors face-to-face with the people who have shaped history, entertainment, and culture.

Gatorland

Gatorland, often referred to as the "Alligator Capital of the World," is a unique wildlife park and attraction located in Orlando, Florida. Established in 1949, Gatorland offers visitors an opportunity to see thousands of alligators and crocodiles, along with a variety of other animals, in a safe and educational environment. The park spans over 110 acres and provides a range of interactive experiences, making it a popular destination for families and wildlife enthusiasts.

One of Gatorland's most popular attractions is the Gator Jumparoo Show, where guests can watch as massive alligators leap out of the water to snatch food from the hands of brave trainers. The park also features the Alligator Breeding Marsh, home to hundreds of alligators in a naturalistic setting complete with boardwalks and observation towers, offering a unique vantage point for observing these incredible creatures in action. Additionally, Gatorland offers the opportunity for up-close encounters with other wildlife, including birds, snakes, and tortoises.

For the more adventurous, Gatorland offers the Screamin' Gator Zip Line, a thrilling ride that takes visitors high above the park, providing stunning aerial views of the alligator and crocodile habitats below. The park also hosts a variety of educational programs and animal shows that highlight the importance of conservation and the role these animals play in the ecosystem.

Gatorland's emphasis on education and conservation, combined with its entertaining and interactive exhibits, make it a unique and memorable attraction in Orlando. Whether you're looking to learn more about Florida's native wildlife or seeking an adrenaline rush, Gatorland offers a one-of-a-kind experience that appeals to visitors of all ages.

Old Town Kissimmee

Old Town Kissimmee is a charming and nostalgic entertainment district located just minutes away from Orlando's major theme parks. Designed to evoke the classic American small town experience, Old Town features a delightful mix of retro-themed shops, restaurants, amusement rides, and live entertainment. Visitors are immediately transported back in time as they stroll down brick-lined streets lined with vintage storefronts, each offering unique wares ranging from quirky souvenirs to old-fashioned candies.

One of Old Town's main attractions is its collection of classic amusement rides, including the iconic Ferris wheel that provides a scenic view of the surrounding area. The district also features a haunted house, bumper cars, and a variety of carnival-style games that appeal to all ages. On weekends, Old Town comes alive with its famous car shows and weekly events. The "Classic Car Show and Cruise," held every Saturday night, is a highlight, drawing car enthusiasts from all over to showcase and admire vintage vehicles as they cruise down Main Street.

In addition to its attractions, Old Town offers a variety of dining options, ranging from casual eateries to themed restaurants. Whether enjoying a meal, shopping for unique gifts, or simply taking in the nostalgic ambiance, Old Town Kissimmee offers a fun and laid-back experience for visitors looking to step back in time and enjoy a slice of Americana.

The Escape Game Orlando

The Escape Game Orlando is a premier destination for immersive and interactive entertainment, offering a series of escape room adventures that challenge participants to solve puzzles, uncover clues, and work together to "escape" from a themed room within a set time limit. Located on International Drive, this attraction is perfect for groups of friends, families, or team-building events, providing an adrenaline-pumping experience that combines mental challenges with physical interaction.

Each escape room at The Escape Game Orlando features a unique theme and storyline, ranging from thrilling heists to daring prison breaks to mysterious adventures. Some of the most popular rooms include "The Heist," where participants must recover a stolen painting from a high-security museum, and "Prison Break," which challenges players to escape from a 1950s prison before the warden returns. Another favorite is

"Mission: Mars," where players must repair their spaceship and escape the Red Planet before time runs out.

The rooms are meticulously designed with detailed sets, props, and special effects that create a highly immersive environment. Players must use their wits, observation skills, and teamwork to solve a series of interconnected puzzles, with the clock ticking down to increase the tension and excitement.

The Escape Game Orlando stands out for its high-quality production values and the creativity of its puzzles, making it a top choice for escape room enthusiasts and newcomers alike. Whether you're looking for a fun challenge or a unique way to bond with friends and family, The Escape Game Orlando offers an unforgettable experience that combines adventure, mystery, and excitement in a single hour of intense, interactive entertainment.

iFLY Orlando

iFLY Orlando offers an exhilarating indoor skydiving experience that allows participants to enjoy the sensation of freefalling without having to jump out of an airplane. Located on International Drive, iFLY Orlando features a state-of-the-art vertical wind tunnel that simulates the feeling of skydiving by creating a powerful updraft, enabling flyers to float effortlessly in the air. This unique attraction is designed for people of all ages and skill levels, making it an accessible and thrilling adventure for everyone.

The experience at iFLY begins with a brief training session led by a certified instructor, where participants learn the basics of body positioning, hand signals, and safety procedures. After suiting up in flight gear, including a helmet, jumpsuit, and goggles, guests enter the wind tunnel for their flight session. Under the guidance of the instructor, flyers experience the sensation of weightlessness as they hover and spin in the air, all while safely contained within the vertical tunnel.

iFLY Orlando is a popular choice for those seeking an adrenaline rush or looking to try something new. It's also a great option for group events, such as birthday parties, corporate team-building, or even just a fun outing with friends and family. The facility also offers advanced training sessions for those who want to develop their flying skills further, as well as virtual reality experiences that combine the thrill of indoor skydiving with the immersive visuals of iconic skydiving locations. With its blend of excitement, innovation, and accessibility, iFLY Orlando provides a memorable experience that lets everyone feel the thrill of flight.

Andretti Indoor Karting & Games

Andretti Indoor Karting & Games in Orlando is a premier entertainment complex that offers a wide range of activities for thrill-seekers and families alike. Named after the legendary race car driver Mario Andretti, the venue is best known for its high-speed indoor go-kart racing, which provides an adrenaline-fueled experience on a professionally designed track. The electric go-karts at Andretti Indoor Karting & Games are capable of reaching impressive speeds, giving both novice and experienced drivers the chance to test their racing skills in a safe and controlled environment.

Beyond karting, Andretti Indoor Karting & Games features a variety of other attractions that cater to different interests. The complex boasts a state-of-the-art arcade with the latest video games and interactive experiences, as well as a multi-level laser tag arena that offers fast-paced action in a futuristic setting. For those seeking a more immersive experience, the venue also includes a cutting-edge virtual reality (VR) zone where guests can explore different worlds and scenarios in full 360-degree environments.

In addition to its core attractions, Andretti Indoor Karting & Games offers boutique bowling lanes, a high ropes course, and a 7D interactive motion theater that combines ride simulation with gaming. The facility also has a full-service restaurant and bar, making it a great spot to relax and refuel between activities.

Whether you're a racing enthusiast, a gamer, or just looking for a fun day out, Andretti Indoor Karting & Games provides a diverse array of entertainment options under one roof, ensuring an exciting experience for all visitors

Shopping and Entertainment Districts

Disney Springs

Disney Springs, located at the Walt Disney World Resort in Orlando, is a vibrant shopping, dining, and entertainment district that offers a mix of experiences for visitors of all ages. Formerly known as Downtown Disney, Disney Springs has been transformed into a dynamic area with four distinct neighborhoods: The Landing, Marketplace, West Side, and Town Center, each offering its own unique atmosphere and attractions.

The Landing is known for its waterfront dining and upscale restaurants. Here, visitors can enjoy meals at renowned establishments like The BOATHOUSE, where you can dine on fresh seafood while watching vintage amphicars cruise by, or at Morimoto Asia, a pan-Asian restaurant by Iron Chef Masaharu Morimoto. The Edison, a steampunk-themed restaurant and bar, offers a blend of American cuisine, craft cocktails, and nightly entertainment, including live music and burlesque shows.

The Marketplace is a haven for Disney fans, featuring iconic stores like World of Disney, the largest Disney character store in the world, and the LEGO Store, where families can build and play with LEGO bricks. The Marketplace is also home to unique dining options like the Rainforest Café and the Ghirardelli Soda Fountain & Chocolate Shop.

West Side is the district's entertainment hub, offering experiences like the AMC Dine-In Theatres, where you can watch the latest movies with in-theater dining service, and the Cirque du Soleil show, "Drawn to Life," which blends acrobatics with Disney animation in a breathtaking performance. The area also features House of Blues, a popular venue for live music, and the NBA Experience, an interactive attraction that immerses visitors in the world of professional basketball.

Town Center is the newest addition to Disney Springs, designed to resemble a Mediterranean-style village. It's the primary shopping destination within Disney Springs, offering a mix of luxury brands and popular retailers such as Zara, Sephora, and Uniqlo. The area also boasts numerous dining options, including fast-casual eateries and fine dining establishments, making it an ideal spot for a leisurely day of shopping and dining.

27

With its combination of world-class dining, unique shopping experiences, and diverse entertainment options, Disney Springs is a must-visit destination for anyone visiting the Orlando area, whether you're a Disney enthusiast or just looking for a memorable day out.

Universal CityWalk

Universal CityWalk in Orlando is a bustling entertainment complex located at the entrance to Universal Orlando Resort, serving as a vibrant gateway to the resort's theme parks. Known as "The Epicenter of Awesome," CityWalk is home to a diverse array of restaurants, shops, and entertainment venues, making it a popular destination for both day and night activities.

CityWalk offers a wide range of dining experiences, catering to every palate. For a taste of classic American cuisine, visitors can head to Hard Rock Cafe, the largest in the world, where they can enjoy burgers and live music surrounded by rock 'n' roll memorabilia. For a more tropical vibe, Margaritaville offers a laid-back atmosphere with Caribbean-inspired dishes and the famous "Cheeseburger in Paradise." Other dining highlights include the Italian-inspired Vivo Italian Kitchen, the vibrant Antojitos Authentic Mexican Food, and the modern fusion cuisine at The Cowfish, known for its "Burgushi" – a creative blend of burgers and sushi.

In addition to its culinary offerings, CityWalk is a hub for entertainment. The area boasts multiple live performance venues, including the world-famous Blue Man Group, whose show combines music, comedy, and multimedia theatrics in an unforgettable experience. CityWalk is also home to the Universal Cineplex, a state-of-the-art movie theater showing the latest blockbusters in IMAX and 3D. For those looking for some after-hours fun, CityWalk features several nightclubs and bars, such as Rising Star, where guests can perform karaoke with a live band, and Pat O'Brien's, a New Orleans-style dueling piano bar.

Shopping at CityWalk is equally diverse, with stores ranging from the Universal Studios Store, where guests can purchase souvenirs and themed merchandise, to specialty shops like the Quiet Flight Surf Shop, catering to surf and skate enthusiasts. For something sweet, Voodoo Doughnut offers an eclectic selection of gourmet doughnuts, each as unique as the vibrant surroundings of CityWalk.

Whether you're starting your day before heading into the theme parks or looking for a lively night out, Universal CityWalk provides a dynamic mix of dining, shopping, and entertainment that appeals to visitors of all ages. Its energetic atmosphere and variety of options make it a key part of the Universal Orlando experience.

Orlando International Premium Outlets

Orlando International Premium Outlets is one of the largest and most popular shopping destinations in Central Florida, attracting millions of visitors each year. Located conveniently on International Drive, this expansive outdoor shopping center features over 180 stores, offering a wide range of products from high-end designer labels to popular everyday brands, all at significant discounts.

The outlets are known for their impressive selection of luxury brands, including names like Coach, Michael Kors, and Burberry, where shoppers can find high-quality fashion and accessories at a fraction of the original retail price. In addition to these designer stores, the outlets offer a variety of popular retail brands such as Nike, Adidas, and Under Armour, catering to those looking for athletic wear and gear. Shoppers can also explore an array of stores offering everything from apparel and footwear to electronics and home goods, with retailers like Tommy Hilfiger, Polo Ralph Lauren, and Calvin Klein drawing particularly large crowds.

The layout of Orlando International Premium Outlets is designed to make shopping easy and enjoyable. The center features wide, well-maintained walkways, outdoor seating areas, and a variety of food options, including quick bites and sit-down restaurants where shoppers can take a break and refuel. For international visitors, the outlets offer a currency exchange service and multilingual staff to assist with any needs, ensuring a seamless shopping experience.

In addition to the regular store discounts, Orlando International Premium Outlets frequently hosts special sales events, where shoppers can find even deeper discounts on already reduced items. The outlets also offer a VIP Shopper Club, providing members with exclusive deals, coupons, and additional savings opportunities.

With its extensive selection of stores, convenient location, and reputation for great deals, Orlando International Premium Outlets is a must-visit destination for both locals and tourists looking to indulge in a day of shopping. Whether you're searching for the latest fashion trends, looking to score a great deal on designer goods, or simply enjoying a leisurely day out, this shopping center offers something for everyone.

Mall at Millenia

The Mall at Millenia is Orlando's premier shopping destination, renowned for its upscale atmosphere and a carefully curated selection of high-end retailers. Located just minutes from the major theme parks, this luxurious, modern shopping center attracts both locals and tourists looking for a world-class shopping experience. The Mall at Millenia is architecturally stunning, with its sleek design featuring skylights, glass elevators, and marble flooring that contribute to an elegant and inviting environment.

The mall is home to an impressive lineup of luxury brands and designer boutiques, including Chanel, Louis Vuitton, Gucci, and Tiffany & Co., making it a must-visit destination for those seeking the latest in fashion and accessories. In addition to these high-end stores, the mall also features popular mainstream retailers such as Apple, Zara, and Anthropologie, providing a well-rounded shopping experience that caters to a variety of tastes and budgets.

Dining at The Mall at Millenia is equally diverse and sophisticated. Shoppers can indulge in fine dining at restaurants like The Capital Grille, known for its steakhouse classics, or enjoy contemporary Italian cuisine at Brio Tuscan Grille. For a more casual bite, the mall's food court offers a range of options, from quick snacks to international cuisine.

The Mall at Millenia also offers a variety of services to enhance the shopping experience, including personal shopping assistance, valet parking, and a concierge desk that provides information on local attractions and events. With its combination of luxury, convenience, and impeccable service, The Mall at Millenia stands out as one of Orlando's top shopping destinations, offering an unparalleled experience for those looking to shop, dine, and relax in style.

Church Street Station

Church Street Station, located in the heart of downtown Orlando, is a historic entertainment district that has played a significant role in the city's cultural and social life for decades. Originally built in the 1880s as a railroad depot, Church Street Station has been transformed over the years into a lively hub of restaurants, bars, and entertainment venues, while retaining its rich historical charm.

The area is best known for its vibrant nightlife, offering a mix of trendy bars, live music venues, and nightclubs that draw crowds of locals and tourists alike. Venues like Latitudes, a popular rooftop bar with sweeping views of downtown Orlando, and The Chiller's, known for its laid-back vibe and frozen drinks, are staples of the Church Street scene. Live music can often be heard spilling out onto the streets, with performances ranging from local bands to nationally recognized artists.

In addition to its nightlife, Church Street Station is also home to a variety of dining options. From casual eateries to upscale restaurants, the area offers something for every palate. Popular spots include The Rusty Spoon, known for its farm-to-table cuisine, and Hamburger Mary's, a lively restaurant famous for its drag performances and comfort food.

Church Street Station's historic architecture adds to its unique atmosphere, with preserved buildings and cobblestone streets providing a charming backdrop for the modern entertainment offerings. The district is also a popular spot for events, from street festivals to holiday celebrations, making it a dynamic and ever-evolving destination.

Whether you're looking to enjoy a night out, dine at some of Orlando's best restaurants, or simply take in the historic ambiance, Church Street Station offers a quintessential downtown experience that captures the spirit of Orlando's past and present.

Historic Downtown Winter Garden

Historic Downtown Winter Garden is a picturesque and charming area located just west of Orlando, offering visitors a glimpse into the region's rich history along with a vibrant community atmosphere. Founded in the early 1900s, Winter Garden was once a bustling center for the citrus industry, and today it has been beautifully preserved and revitalized, blending its historic roots with modern amenities and attractions.

The heart of Downtown Winter Garden is Plant Street, lined with brick-paved sidewalks, historic buildings, and a variety of unique shops, restaurants, and cultural venues. The area is known for its friendly, small-town vibe, making it a popular destination for locals and visitors looking for a relaxing day out. Specialty boutiques, such as Adjectives Market and

31

The Ancient Olive, offer a variety of artisanal goods, antiques, and gourmet products that make for perfect souvenirs or gifts.

Dining in Historic Downtown Winter Garden is a treat, with a range of options that cater to all tastes. The Chef's Table at the Edgewater, an award-winning fine dining restaurant, offers a gourmet experience in an intimate setting, while more casual eateries like Axum Coffee and Winter Garden Pizza Company provide a laid-back atmosphere for enjoying a meal or coffee with friends.

The district is also a cultural hub, home to the historic Garden Theatre, a beautifully restored venue that hosts a variety of performances, including plays, musicals, and film screenings. The Winter Garden Heritage Museum offers visitors a look into the area's history, with exhibits that explore the town's citrus industry past and its development over the years.

One of the highlights of visiting Historic Downtown Winter Garden is the weekly Farmers Market, held every Saturday. The market is a local favorite, offering fresh produce, handmade crafts, and live entertainment in a festive outdoor setting.

With its rich history, vibrant community, and welcoming atmosphere, Historic Downtown Winter Garden provides a perfect blend of past and present, making it an ideal destination for a leisurely day of shopping, dining, and exploring in Central Florida.

Museums and Cultural Attractions

Orlando Museum of Art

The Orlando Museum of Art (OMA) is one of Central Florida's premier cultural institutions, offering a dynamic array of exhibitions, programs, and events that celebrate visual art from around the world. Founded in 1924, the museum is located in the beautiful Loch Haven Park, making it a central part of Orlando's cultural landscape. The OMA's mission is to inspire creativity, passion, and intellectual curiosity by providing innovative and engaging art experiences for visitors of all ages.

The museum's permanent collection features over 2,400 works of art, spanning a wide range of periods and styles. This includes American art from the 18th to the 20th century, contemporary art, African art, and art of the ancient Americas. The OMA is particularly noted for its collection of contemporary art, which includes works by significant artists such as Georgia O'Keeffe, Ansel Adams, and Robert Rauschenberg. The museum also regularly hosts traveling exhibitions, which bring internationally renowned artworks to Orlando, allowing visitors to experience a diverse array of artistic expressions.

In addition to its exhibitions, the Orlando Museum of Art offers a variety of educational programs designed to engage the community and foster a deeper appreciation for the arts. These include art classes, workshops, and lectures, as well as special programs for children and families. The museum's "1st Thursdays" event is a popular monthly gathering that showcases local artists, live music, and food and drink, creating a vibrant and social atmosphere for art lovers.

The OMA's commitment to both showcasing significant artworks and nurturing local talent makes it a vital part of Orlando's cultural scene. Whether you're a seasoned art aficionado or simply looking for an inspiring way to spend an afternoon, the Orlando Museum of Art offers a rich and rewarding experience that highlights the power of art to connect, inspire, and transform.

Charles Hosmer Morse Museum of American Art

The Charles Hosmer Morse Museum of American Art, located in Winter Park, Florida, is home to the world's most comprehensive collection of works by Louis Comfort Tiffany, including his iconic stained glass, jewelry, pottery, and paintings. Established in 1942, the museum was named after Charles Hosmer Morse, a Chicago industrialist and philanthropist who was a major benefactor of the arts. The museum's collection was assembled by his granddaughter, Jeannette Genius McKean, and her husband, Hugh F. McKean, who served as the museum's director for many years.

The museum's centerpiece is its extensive collection of Tiffany's work, which includes examples of his renowned leaded-glass lamps, windows, and mosaics. One of the highlights is the restored chapel interior that Tiffany designed for the 1893 World's Columbian Exposition in Chicago. This stunning exhibit includes the chapel's original stained-glass windows, intricate mosaics, and a bronze and glass altar, offering visitors a breathtaking example of Tiffany's artistry and craftsmanship.

In addition to the Tiffany collection, the Morse Museum features an impressive array of American decorative arts from the late 19th and early 20th centuries. This includes ceramics, paintings, furniture, and textiles, which together provide a rich context for understanding the broader American art movements of the period. The museum's galleries are carefully curated to showcase the beauty and innovation of American art and design, with each room offering a unique and immersive experience.

The Charles Hosmer Morse Museum of American Art is more than just a collection of beautiful objects; it's a testament to the vision and creativity of Louis Comfort Tiffany and his contemporaries. Whether you're a fan of decorative arts, a history enthusiast, or simply someone who appreciates beauty, a visit to the Morse Museum offers a deep and enriching experience that celebrates the best of American art and craftsmanship.

Orange County Regional History Center

The Orange County Regional History Center, located in the heart of downtown Orlando, is a vibrant museum dedicated to preserving and presenting the rich history of Central Florida. Housed in a historic courthouse built in 1927, the History Center offers visitors a comprehensive journey through the region's past, from its indigenous beginnings to its rise as a major tourist destination and beyond.

The museum's exhibits are spread across four floors, each offering a unique perspective on different aspects of Central Florida's history. One of the standout exhibits is the "Destination Florida" gallery, which explores the state's transformation into a global tourist hub, driven by the development of theme parks and the rise of the hospitality industry. This exhibit includes fascinating artifacts, photographs, and multimedia displays that capture the excitement and innovation that have shaped the region.

Another significant exhibit is "First People," which delves into the lives and cultures of Florida's indigenous populations, providing insights into their customs, technologies, and interactions with European settlers. The History Center also features exhibits on the pioneer era, the impact of the citrus industry, and the role of Central Florida during the Civil Rights Movement, offering a well-rounded view of the region's development over time.

In addition to its permanent exhibits, the Orange County Regional History Center hosts rotating special exhibitions that highlight various aspects of local and national history. The museum also offers a wide range of educational programs, including guided tours, workshops, and lectures, designed to engage visitors of all ages and foster a deeper understanding of the area's history.

The History Center's commitment to preserving and sharing Central Florida's heritage makes it an essential destination for anyone interested in the region's past. Whether you're a local resident, a history buff, or a tourist looking to learn more about the area, the Orange County Regional History Center offers an informative and engaging experience that connects the past with the present in meaningful ways.

Mennello Museum of American Art

The Mennello Museum of American Art, situated in the picturesque Loch Haven Park in Orlando, is a cultural treasure dedicated to showcasing American art with a particular focus on traditional and contemporary works. Established in 1998, the museum is renowned for its outstanding collection of paintings by Earl Cunningham, a self-taught folk artist whose vibrant and imaginative landscapes capture the essence of rural America. Cunningham's works are the centerpiece of the museum's permanent collection, offering visitors a window into the artist's unique vision of the American landscape.

In addition to Cunningham's paintings, the Mennello Museum hosts rotating exhibitions that feature a diverse range of American artists, from 19th-century masters to contemporary creators. These exhibitions span various media, including painting, sculpture, and photography, providing a comprehensive look at the evolution of American art. The museum's commitment to inclusivity and diversity is reflected in its programming, which often highlights underrepresented artists and offers fresh perspectives on American culture and history.

The museum's serene lakeside setting enhances the visitor experience, with the grounds featuring a beautiful sculpture garden that invites guests to explore and enjoy art in an outdoor environment. The garden includes works by renowned artists such as Alice Aycock and Barbara Sorensen, creating a harmonious blend of nature and art.

The Mennello Museum also plays an active role in the community through educational programs, workshops, and special events that engage audiences of all ages. These initiatives aim to foster a deeper appreciation of American art and provide opportunities for creative expression. Whether you are an art enthusiast or simply looking for a peaceful retreat in the heart of Orlando, the Mennello Museum of American Art offers a rich and inspiring experience.

Albin Polasek Museum & Sculpture Gardens

The Albin Polasek Museum & Sculpture Gardens, located in Winter Park, Florida, is a captivating museum dedicated to the life and work of Albin Polasek, a celebrated Czech-American sculptor. The museum, housed in Polasek's former home and studio, offers a comprehensive look at his prolific career, showcasing a wide array of his sculptures, paintings, and personal artifacts. Born in 1879, Polasek immigrated to the United States, where he became one of the most influential sculptors of the early 20th century, known for his classical and religious-themed works.

Visitors to the museum are greeted by Polasek's stunning sculptures, many of which are displayed in the lush outdoor gardens that surround the property. The gardens are meticulously landscaped and feature over 50 of Polasek's works, including some of his most famous pieces like "Man Carving His Own Destiny" and "The Sower." These sculptures are thoughtfully placed among the gardens' flowers, trees, and serene water features, creating a tranquil environment where art and nature coexist harmoniously.

Inside the museum, visitors can explore Polasek's studio, which has been preserved much as it was during his lifetime. The studio offers a unique insight into the artist's creative process, with unfinished works, tools, and sketches on display. The museum also hosts rotating exhibitions that highlight other artists, particularly those whose work resonates with Polasek's legacy.

In addition to its art collection, the Albin Polasek Museum offers various educational programs, workshops, and events designed to engage the community and promote an appreciation for the arts. Whether you are an art lover or someone seeking a peaceful and inspiring outing, the Albin Polasek Museum & Sculpture Gardens provides a rich cultural experience in a setting of natural beauty.

Orlando Fire Museum

The Orlando Fire Museum, located in the historic Loch Haven Park, is a fascinating destination that offers visitors a glimpse into the history of firefighting in Orlando. Housed in a beautifully restored firehouse that dates back to 1926, the museum preserves and showcases the rich heritage of the Orlando Fire Department and its evolution over the years. This two-story, red-brick building is a historical landmark itself, representing the architectural style and community spirit of early 20th-century Orlando.

Inside the museum, visitors can explore a variety of exhibits that chronicle the history of firefighting, from the early days of horse-drawn fire engines to the modern equipment used today. The collection includes antique fire trucks, helmets, uniforms, and other firefighting gear, offering a hands-on experience that appeals to visitors of all ages. One of the museum's highlights is the 1926 American LaFrance fire engine, meticulously restored and displayed as a centerpiece of the collection.

The museum also features historical photographs, documents, and artifacts that tell the stories of the brave men and women who have served in the Orlando Fire Department over the years. These exhibits provide a deep sense of the challenges and heroism associated with firefighting, offering a powerful tribute to the city's first responders.

In addition to its exhibits, the Orlando Fire Museum engages the community through educational programs, including tours for school groups and special events that celebrate the history of firefighting. The museum is staffed by knowledgeable volunteers, many of whom are retired firefighters, who provide insightful tours and share personal stories that bring the history to life.

The Orlando Fire Museum is a must-visit for anyone interested in history, firefighting, or community heritage. It offers a unique and educational experience that honors the legacy of Orlando's firefighters and their contributions to the safety and well-being of the city.

Holocaust Memorial Resource & Education Center

The Holocaust Memorial Resource & Education Center, located in Maitland, Florida, just outside Orlando, is a vital institution dedicated to educating the public about the Holocaust and promoting human rights and tolerance. Established in 1981, the center was one of the first in the United States to focus on Holocaust education and remembrance. It serves as both a memorial to the victims of the Holocaust and a resource for those seeking to learn about this tragic period in history and its lasting impact on the world.

The center features a permanent exhibition that chronicles the history of the Holocaust through photographs, artifacts, personal narratives, and multimedia presentations. The exhibition provides a comprehensive overview of the events leading up to the Holocaust, the atrocities committed during the genocide, and the experiences of survivors who rebuilt their lives after World War II. One of the most poignant aspects of the exhibition is the collection of personal testimonies from Holocaust survivors, many of whom settled in Florida after the war. These stories provide a powerful and personal connection to history, emphasizing the importance of remembrance and education.

In addition to its permanent exhibition, the Holocaust Memorial Resource & Education Center offers a variety of educational programs, including lectures, film screenings, and workshops aimed at students, educators, and the general public. The center also hosts special exhibitions that explore related themes such as genocide, human rights, and social justice.

The center's mission extends beyond Holocaust remembrance to include a focus on contemporary issues of intolerance, discrimination, and violence. Through its programs and outreach efforts, the center works to foster a culture of respect and understanding, encouraging visitors to reflect on the lessons of the Holocaust and apply them to the challenges of today.

Visiting the Holocaust Memorial Resource & Education Center is a deeply moving and educational experience that underscores the importance of remembering the past to build a more just and compassionate future. Whether you are a student, educator, or concerned citizen, the center offers valuable insights and resources that contribute to a greater understanding of human rights and the ongoing fight against hatred and bigotry.

Wells' Built Museum of African American History & Culture

The Wells' Built Museum of African American History & Culture, located in the historic Parramore district of Orlando, is a vital institution dedicated to preserving and celebrating the rich history and contributions of African Americans in Central Florida. The museum is housed in what was once the Wells' Built Hotel, a landmark establishment built in 1926 by Dr. William Monroe Wells, one of Orlando's first African American physicians. During the segregation era, the hotel provided accommodations to African American travelers, including musicians, athletes, and entertainers who were barred from staying in white-owned hotels.

The museum's exhibits provide a comprehensive look at the African American experience in Orlando and beyond, with a focus on the struggles and achievements of the local community. Visitors can explore a range of artifacts, photographs, and documents that tell the stories of the people who lived and worked in the Parramore district. Highlights include memorabilia from the Civil Rights Movement, vintage musical instruments, and displays that highlight the cultural significance of the hotel as a hub for social and cultural activities during its heyday.

One of the most poignant aspects of the museum is its collection of photographs and oral histories that capture the resilience and determination of the African American community in the face of discrimination and adversity. The museum also features a re-creation of a typical guest room from the Wells' Built Hotel, offering visitors a glimpse into the past and the conditions under which travelers stayed.

The Wells' Built Museum is more than just a repository of history; it serves as a cultural center that hosts events, lectures, and performances that celebrate African American culture and heritage. Through its exhibits and programs, the museum plays a crucial role in educating the public and preserving the legacy of the African American community in Central Florida.

Cornell Fine Arts Museum

The Cornell Fine Arts Museum, located on the campus of Rollins College in Winter Park, Florida, is a distinguished institution that offers visitors an exceptional collection of artworks spanning from antiquity to the contemporary era. Founded in 1942, the museum serves as a cultural and educational resource for both the college and the broader community, providing a space where art, history, and culture intersect.

The museum's collection is notably diverse, featuring over 5,500 works of art, including paintings, sculptures, photographs, and decorative arts. Among its most significant holdings are works by Old Masters such as Jusepe de Ribera and Sir Joshua Reynolds, as well as pieces by modern and contemporary artists like Henri Matisse, Andy Warhol, and Kara Walker. The museum also boasts an impressive array of American art, with notable works by artists such as Thomas Moran and Georgia O'Keeffe.

In addition to its permanent collection, the Cornell Fine Arts Museum regularly hosts temporary exhibitions that explore various themes and movements in art history. These exhibitions often include works on loan from other prestigious institutions, providing visitors with the opportunity to experience a wide range of artistic expressions. The museum's commitment to education is reflected in its robust schedule of public programs, which include lectures, workshops, and guided tours designed to engage visitors of all ages.

The museum's location on the scenic Rollins College campus adds to the visitor experience, with the nearby Lake Virginia providing a tranquil backdrop for the contemplation of art. The museum also operates the Alfond Collection of Contemporary Art at The Alfond Inn, a unique extension of its programming that integrates art into the hotel's public spaces.

The Cornell Fine Arts Museum is a cornerstone of the cultural life in Winter Park, offering a rich and varied experience that appeals to art enthusiasts, scholars, and casual visitors alike. Its dedication to preserving and presenting works of art in a scholarly and accessible manner makes it an invaluable resource for the community.

Zora Neale Hurston National Museum of Fine Arts

The Zora Neale Hurston National Museum of Fine Arts, often referred to as "The Hurston," is a cultural landmark located in Eatonville, Florida, the oldest incorporated African American municipality in the United States. Named after the celebrated author and anthropologist Zora Neale Hurston, who spent her formative years in Eatonville, the museum honors her legacy by promoting the work of artists of African descent and celebrating the cultural contributions of African Americans.

The Hurston is a small but significant museum that serves as a hub for African American art, history, and culture. The museum primarily focuses on contemporary African American art, featuring rotating exhibitions that showcase the work of both emerging and established artists. These exhibitions cover a wide range of media, including painting, sculpture, photography, and mixed media, reflecting the diversity and richness of African American artistic expression.

One of the museum's key missions is to highlight the contributions of African American artists who have been historically underrepresented in mainstream art institutions. The Hurston's exhibitions often explore themes related to the African American experience, such as identity, heritage, social justice, and community. By providing a platform for these artists, the museum plays a crucial role in fostering a deeper understanding and appreciation of African American culture.

In addition to its exhibitions, The Hurston is actively involved in the community, hosting educational programs, workshops, and events that engage local residents and visitors alike. The museum is also a central part of the annual Zora Neale Hurston Festival of the Arts and Humanities, a major cultural event that attracts scholars, artists, and visitors from across the country to celebrate Hurston's life and work.

Visiting The Hurston offers a unique opportunity to connect with the legacy of one of America's most influential literary figures while exploring the vibrant art and culture of the African American community. The museum stands as a testament to the enduring impact of Zora Neale Hurston and her contributions to American literature and culture.

The Winter Park Historical Museum, located in the heart of Winter Park, Florida, is a charming institution dedicated to preserving and sharing the rich history of this picturesque community. Founded in 1970, the museum offers visitors a fascinating glimpse into the past, chronicling the development of Winter Park from its early days as a small resort town to its present status as a vibrant and culturally rich city.

The museum's exhibits are thoughtfully curated to reflect the unique character and heritage of Winter Park. Permanent displays include artifacts, photographs, and documents that tell the story of the town's founding in the late 19th century, its growth as a winter retreat for wealthy Northerners, and its evolution into a thriving cultural hub. The museum also highlights the contributions of key figures in Winter Park's history, such as Loring Chase and Oliver Chapman, the town's founders, and Charles Hosmer Morse, whose philanthropy helped shape the community.

One of the museum's most popular exhibits focuses on the Winter Park train station, a historic landmark that played a crucial role in the town's development. The exhibit features memorabilia from the golden age of rail travel, including vintage tickets, timetables, and photographs, providing a nostalgic look at how the railroad connected Winter Park to the broader world.

In addition to its permanent exhibits, the Winter Park Historical Museum hosts rotating exhibitions that delve into various aspects of local history, from the architecture of Winter Park's historic homes to the town's cultural and artistic achievements. The museum also plays an active role in the community, offering educational programs, lectures, and walking tours that engage both residents and visitors in exploring the town's rich history.

The Winter Park Historical Museum is more than just a repository of artifacts; it is a vibrant center for learning and community engagement. By preserving and sharing the stories of Winter Park's past, the museum helps to foster a deeper appreciation for the town's heritage and contributes to the ongoing sense of pride and identity among its residents. Whether you are a history enthusiast or simply curious about the origins of this charming community, the Winter Park Historical Museum offers a rewarding and educational experience.

The Harry T. & Harriette V. Moore Memorial Park & Museum, located in Mims, Florida, is a deeply significant site dedicated to the lives and legacy of two pioneering civil rights activists, Harry T. Moore and his wife, Harriette V. Moore. The Moores were among the earliest leaders of the modern civil rights movement, advocating tirelessly for racial equality, voter rights, and the end of segregation in the Jim Crow South. Their courageous work laid the foundation for the broader civil rights movement that would follow, but tragically, their activism also made them targets of racial violence. On Christmas night in 1951, the Moores' home was bombed, resulting in the deaths of both Harry and Harriette, marking the first assassination of civil rights leaders in the United States.

The Memorial Park & Museum serves as both a tribute to their legacy and an educational resource that sheds light on the history of civil rights in America. The museum features a range of exhibits that document the Moores' lives, their activism, and the broader social and political context of their work. Visitors can explore photographs, documents, and artifacts that illustrate the challenges they faced and the impact of their efforts in advancing civil rights.

One of the key features of the site is a replica of the Moores' home, meticulously recreated to reflect the conditions of their life and work in the early 1950s. This provides visitors with a tangible connection to the past, offering a sense of the personal and physical environment in which the Moores carried out their courageous work.

The surrounding park includes a reflective pond, a civil rights trail, and a memorial plaza that honors the Moores and other civil rights martyrs. The serene environment encourages contemplation and remembrance, making it a powerful space for reflection on the ongoing struggle for justice and equality.

Through its exhibits, programs, and events, the Harry T. & Harriette V. Moore Memorial Park & Museum not only preserves the memory of these two remarkable individuals but also educates future generations about the history of civil rights in America. It stands as a poignant reminder of the sacrifices made in the fight for equality and the enduring importance of their work in the ongoing quest for social justice.

The Orlando Science Center

The Orlando Science Center is a premier destination for education and entertainment in Orlando, Florida. Established to inspire curiosity and encourage a love for science, this hands-on museum offers a wide range of exhibits and programs suitable for all ages. Located in Loch Haven Park, the Orlando Science Center has been a staple in the community since its founding, providing a dynamic environment where visitors can explore the wonders of science and technology.

One of the center's highlights is its interactive exhibits, which cover various topics, from physics and biology to environmental science and engineering. Exhibits like "Our Planet, Our Universe" offer an immersive look into the cosmos and Earth's unique ecosystems, while "KidsTown" is a favorite among younger visitors, offering a space where children can engage in creative play and learn about the world around them.

The Orlando Science Center also features live programming, including science demonstrations, workshops, and educational films in the Dr. Phillips CineDome. The dome's giant screen provides an awe-inspiring venue for learning about the natural world, space exploration, and more.

Additionally, the center houses an observatory equipped with powerful telescopes, allowing visitors to explore the night sky and learn about astronomy. Special events like "Science Night Live" offer adults a chance to explore the exhibits with a different twist, often featuring guest speakers, live shows, and themed activities.

Overall, the Orlando Science Center is a place where science comes to life, making it a must-visit for both locals and tourists interested in discovery and lifelong learning.

Natural and Outdoor Attractions

Lake Eola Park

Lake Eola Park, located in downtown Orlando, Florida, is a beautiful urban oasis that offers a serene escape from the city's hustle and bustle. The park is centered around Lake Eola, a picturesque lake known for its iconic fountain, which illuminates at night, creating a stunning visual display. Covering 43 acres, Lake Eola Park is a popular destination for both locals and tourists, offering a variety of recreational activities and scenic views.

Visitors can enjoy a leisurely stroll along the park's one-mile walking path that circles the lake, offering picturesque views of Orlando's skyline and opportunities to spot swans, ducks, and other wildlife. The park is also famous for its swan boats, which can be rented for a unique experience of paddling around the lake. In addition to its natural beauty, Lake Eola Park hosts a variety of events throughout the year, including the Orlando Farmers Market, cultural festivals, concerts, and outdoor movies, making it a vibrant community hub.

The Walt Disney Amphitheater, located within the park, is a popular venue for live performances and special events. The park also features playgrounds, picnic areas, and a Chinese pagoda, adding to its charm and appeal. Lake Eola Park is not just a place for relaxation and recreation; it's a cultural landmark in Orlando, reflecting the city's vibrant community spirit. Whether enjoying a peaceful day on the water, attending a local event, or simply taking in the beautiful surroundings, Lake Eola Park offers something for everyone.

Harry P. Leu Gardens

Harry P. Leu Gardens, located near downtown Orlando, is a lush, 50-acre botanical oasis that offers visitors a tranquil retreat from the urban hustle. Established in 1961, the gardens were originally the estate of Harry P. Leu, a successful businessman and philanthropist who, along with his wife, Mary Jane, collected plants and trees from around the world to create a stunning horticultural showcase. Today, the gardens are operated by the City of Orlando and are open to the public year-round.

Leu Gardens are known for their extensive collection of tropical and subtropical plants, including more than 240 varieties of camellias, making it one of the most significant camellia collections in the southeastern United States. Visitors can also explore themed gardens, such as the Rose Garden, Palm Garden, and Butterfly Garden, each offering its own unique beauty and appeal. The sprawling oak trees draped in Spanish moss and the serene lake views add to the garden's charm, creating a peaceful environment perfect for relaxation and reflection.

The historic Leu House Museum, located on the grounds, provides a glimpse into early 20th-century Florida life. The home, which is listed on the National Register of Historic Places, offers guided tours that share the history of the Leu family and the evolution of the gardens.

In addition to its horticultural beauty, Leu Gardens hosts a variety of events and educational programs throughout the year, including gardening workshops, plant sales, and seasonal festivals. The gardens also serve as a popular venue for weddings and special events, offering a picturesque setting for memorable occasions.

Harry P. Leu Gardens is a must-visit destination for nature lovers, horticulture enthusiasts, and anyone seeking a serene escape in the heart of Orlando. Its combination of natural beauty, historical significance, and educational opportunities makes it a cherished part of Central Florida's cultural landscape.

Bok Tower Gardens

Bok Tower Gardens, located in Lake Wales, Florida, is a breathtakingly beautiful sanctuary that blends nature, art, and music into a serene and inspiring experience. Established in 1929 by Edward W. Bok, a Pulitzer Prize-winning author and humanitarian, the gardens were created as a gift to the American people to express Bok's gratitude for the opportunities he found in the United States. The centerpiece of the gardens is the majestic Singing Tower, a 205-foot neo-Gothic and art deco structure that houses one of the world's finest carillons, a musical instrument consisting of 60 bronze bells.

The gardens themselves are a masterpiece of landscape design, created by the famous landscape architect Frederick Law Olmsted Jr., who is also known for his work on the National Mall in Washington, D.C. Covering over 250 acres, the gardens feature a variety of plantings, including azaleas, camellias, and magnolias, as well as native plants that attract a diverse array of wildlife. The lush, rolling hills, tranquil reflection pools, and scenic vistas provide a perfect setting for quiet contemplation and exploration.

Visitors to Bok Tower Gardens can enjoy daily carillon concerts, where the melodic chimes of the Singing Tower resonate through the gardens, creating an ethereal atmosphere that enhances the natural beauty of the surroundings. The Pinewood Estate, a historic 1930s Mediterranean-style mansion located on the property, offers guided tours that showcase its exquisite architecture and furnishings.

In addition to its natural and architectural beauty, Bok Tower Gardens hosts various educational programs, workshops, and seasonal events, including concerts, garden tours, and holiday celebrations. The gardens also offer miles of walking trails, picnic areas, and a visitor center with exhibits about the history and significance of the site.

Bok Tower Gardens is a tranquil retreat that provides a perfect escape from the everyday hustle, offering visitors a unique blend of nature, culture, and history. It stands as a testament to Edward Bok's vision of creating a place of beauty and peace for all to enjoy.

Lake Apopka Wildlife Drive

Lake Apopka Wildlife Drive is a hidden gem in Central Florida, offering nature enthusiasts and birdwatchers an opportunity to explore one of the state's most ecologically rich environments from the comfort of their own vehicle. Located on the northern shore of Lake Apopka, the drive is an 11-mile one-way route that winds through the Lake Apopka North Shore, a vast restoration area managed by the St. Johns River Water Management District.

The drive provides visitors with an up-close look at the diverse habitats that make up this area, including wetlands, marshes, and flatwoods. These ecosystems support an incredible variety of wildlife, making it one of the premier birdwatching spots in Florida. Over 360 species of birds have been documented in the area, including herons, egrets, ospreys, and even the rare and elusive whooping crane. In addition to birdlife, visitors can often spot alligators basking in the sun, as well as otters, turtles, and other wildlife.

One of the key attractions of the Lake Apopka Wildlife Drive is the ability to experience nature at your own pace. Visitors can drive slowly through the area, stopping at designated pull-offs to observe wildlife, take photographs, or simply enjoy the peaceful surroundings. Informational signs along the route provide insights into the area's history, the restoration efforts to revive the lake and its ecosystems, and the types of wildlife you might encounter.

The drive is open on weekends and federal holidays, and admission is free, making it an accessible and affordable outing for families, nature lovers, and photographers alike. The route is well-maintained, and restrooms are available at the entrance, ensuring a comfortable experience for all visitors.

Lake Apopka Wildlife Drive offers a unique opportunity to connect with Florida's natural beauty and observe wildlife in their natural habitat. It's a perfect escape for those looking to enjoy a serene and immersive experience in the great outdoors.

Winter Park Scenic Boat Tour

The Winter Park Scenic Boat Tour is a quintessential Central Florida experience that offers visitors a unique perspective on the charm and beauty of Winter Park. Established in 1938, this guided boat tour takes passengers on an hour-long journey through the scenic lakes and historic canals of Winter Park, providing a relaxing and informative way to explore the area's natural and architectural splendor.

The tour departs from the dock on Lake Osceola, one of the five interconnected lakes that make up the Winter Park Chain of Lakes. As the pontoon boat glides across the water, passengers are treated to breathtaking views of lush landscapes, elegant mansions, and historic landmarks. The knowledgeable tour guides share fascinating stories and facts about the area's history, pointing out notable sites such as Rollins College, Kraft Azalea Gardens, and the grand estates that line the shores of the lakes.

One of the highlights of the tour is the passage through the narrow, man-made canals that connect the lakes. These picturesque waterways, bordered by towering cypress trees and tropical foliage, provide a serene and intimate setting that feels worlds away from the hustle and bustle of nearby Orlando. The canals were originally built in the late 19th and early

20th centuries to facilitate the transport of goods between the lakes, and today they serve as a charming reminder of Winter Park's rich history.

The Winter Park Scenic Boat Tour is popular with both locals and tourists, offering a peaceful escape and a chance to experience the natural beauty of Central Florida in a unique way. Whether you're interested in the history of the area, the stunning architecture, or simply enjoying a leisurely boat ride, this tour provides a memorable experience that showcases the best of Winter Park.

With its combination of natural beauty, historical significance, and expert narration, the Winter Park Scenic Boat Tour is a must-do activity for anyone visiting the area. It offers a perfect blend of relaxation and discovery, making it an ideal way to spend an afternoon in one of Central Florida's most picturesque communities.

Greenwood Cemetery

Greenwood Cemetery, located in the heart of Orlando, is more than just a resting place for the departed; it is a historic site that offers a peaceful retreat and a rich connection to the city's past. Established in 1880, Greenwood Cemetery spans over 120 acres and serves as the final resting place for many of Orlando's most notable citizens, including politicians, veterans, and pioneers who helped shape the city's history.

The cemetery is laid out in a picturesque manner, with rolling hills, winding paths, and mature oak trees draped in Spanish moss, creating a serene and contemplative atmosphere. The carefully maintained grounds are dotted with historic monuments, mausoleums, and headstones, each telling a story of the individuals and families who contributed to the growth and development of Orlando. Notable sections of the cemetery include the graves of veterans from various wars, as well as the historic African American section, which reflects the segregation that once existed even in death.

Greenwood Cemetery is also known for its guided moonlight walking tours, which offer visitors a chance to explore the cemetery after dark while learning about Orlando's history and some of the more famous and infamous individuals buried there. These tours, led by knowledgeable guides, provide fascinating insights into the city's past and the lives of its early residents.

In addition to its historical significance, Greenwood Cemetery is a place of natural beauty and tranquility, offering a quiet space for reflection and remembrance. It is a place where history and nature converge, making it an important part of Orlando's cultural and historical landscape. Whether visiting to pay respects, learn about local history, or simply enjoy a peaceful walk, Greenwood Cemetery provides a unique and meaningful experience.

Lake Ivanhoe Park

Lake Ivanhoe Park, located in the Ivanhoe Village district of Orlando, is a popular urban park that offers a variety of recreational opportunities along the shores of one of the city's most scenic lakes. Known for its picturesque views of downtown Orlando's skyline, the park is a beloved destination for locals and visitors alike, providing a peaceful escape from the hustle and bustle of city life.

The park features a well-maintained walking and biking trail that winds around the lake, offering stunning views of the water and the surrounding greenery. This trail is ideal for jogging, walking, or simply enjoying a leisurely stroll while taking in the natural beauty of the area. The park's expansive green spaces also make it a perfect spot for picnicking, lounging, or playing sports. Families often come to the park to enjoy the playground, which provides a safe and fun environment for children.

One of the key attractions of Lake Ivanhoe Park is its access to Lake Ivanhoe itself, a popular spot for water-based activities. The lake is well-known among paddleboarders, kayakers, and anglers, who enjoy the calm waters and the opportunity to connect with nature just minutes from downtown Orlando. The park also features a boat ramp, making it easy for visitors to launch their own watercraft.

Lake Ivanhoe Park is also a popular venue for community events, such as outdoor concerts, festivals, and yoga classes, which add to the vibrant atmosphere of the surrounding Ivanhoe Village area. The park's scenic backdrop, combined with its recreational amenities, makes it a versatile space that caters to a wide range of interests and activities.

Whether you're looking to exercise, relax, or engage in outdoor activities, Lake Ivanhoe Park offers a perfect blend of urban convenience and natural beauty. Its central location, combined with its tranquil setting, makes it a cherished green space in the heart of Orlando.

Tibet-Butler Preserve

Tibet-Butler Preserve, located in southwest Orlando, is a pristine natural area that offers visitors a chance to experience Florida's unique ecosystems and wildlife up close. Covering approximately 440 acres, the preserve is a sanctuary for a variety of native plants and animals, providing a serene escape from the city and a perfect destination for nature lovers and outdoor enthusiasts.

The preserve features several well-marked hiking trails that wind through diverse habitats, including pine flatwoods, hardwood hammocks, and wetlands. The Osprey Overlook Trail, one of the most popular paths, leads to a scenic boardwalk that extends over Lake Tibet-Butler, offering stunning views of the water and a chance to spot ospreys, herons, and other bird species. The trails are designed to accommodate different skill levels, making the preserve accessible to hikers of all ages and abilities.

Tibet-Butler Preserve is also an excellent destination for birdwatching, with over 100 species of birds recorded in the area. The preserve's diverse habitats support a variety of wildlife, including deer, gopher tortoises, and the occasional alligator. Interpretive signs along the trails provide information about the local flora and fauna, enhancing the educational experience for visitors.

In addition to its natural beauty, the preserve is home to the Vera Carter Environmental Center, which offers interactive exhibits on Central Florida's ecosystems and conservation efforts. The center also hosts educational programs, guided nature walks, and workshops, making it a valuable resource for those interested in learning more about the environment.

Tibet-Butler Preserve is a peaceful and well-preserved natural area that offers a welcome retreat from urban life. Whether you're hiking, birdwatching, or simply enjoying the tranquility of nature, the preserve provides a unique opportunity to connect with Florida's natural heritage.

Wekiwa Springs State Park

Wekiwa Springs State Park, located in Apopka, Florida, just a short drive from Orlando, is a natural paradise that offers a wide range of outdoor activities and a glimpse into Florida's natural beauty. Spanning over 7,000 acres, the park is centered around the crystal-clear Wekiwa Spring, which has been attracting visitors for generations with its refreshing waters and scenic surroundings.

The spring is the park's main attraction, pumping out 42 million gallons of water daily at a consistent temperature of 72 degrees Fahrenheit. Visitors can swim, snorkel, or simply relax in the cool, clear waters, which are surrounded by lush vegetation and shaded by towering trees. The spring also serves as the headwaters for the Wekiva River, a designated National Wild and Scenic River, making it a popular spot for canoeing and kayaking. Paddlers can explore the tranquil river and its winding tributaries, often encountering a variety of wildlife, including manatees, otters, and a diverse array of bird species.

Wekiwa Springs State Park is also a haven for hikers and nature enthusiasts, with more than 13 miles of trails that traverse different ecosystems, from sandhill communities to river swamps. The trails vary in difficulty and length, offering something for everyone, whether you're looking for a short walk or a more challenging hike. The park is also home to an extensive network of equestrian and biking trails, providing additional opportunities for outdoor recreation.

Camping is another popular activity at Wekiwa Springs, with the park offering both primitive and modern campsites. The campgrounds are well-equipped and provide a peaceful setting for an overnight stay surrounded by nature.

The park also offers educational programs, guided tours, and ranger-led activities that highlight the area's natural and cultural history. With its combination of recreational opportunities, scenic beauty, and rich biodiversity, Wekiwa Springs State Park is a must-visit destination for anyone looking to experience the best of Central Florida's natural environment. Whether you're there to swim, paddle, hike, or simply relax, the park offers a rejuvenating escape into nature.

Performing Arts and Entertainment Venues

Dr. Phillips Center for the Performing Arts

The Dr. Phillips Center for the Performing Arts is a premier cultural and entertainment venue located in downtown Orlando, Florida. Opened in 2014, the center has quickly become a key destination for world-class performances, hosting a wide range of events from Broadway shows and concerts to ballet, opera, and comedy acts. The Dr. Phillips Center is known for its state-of-the-art design and acoustics, making it one of the top performing arts venues in the country.

The complex features several performance spaces, including the Walt Disney Theater, the largest hall with seating for over 2,700 guests, known for its stunning architecture and excellent acoustics. The Alexis & Jim Pugh Theater offers a more intimate setting with 300 seats, ideal for smaller performances and community events. The center also includes the Steinmetz Hall, a highly anticipated space designed to accommodate a diverse range of performances with adjustable acoustics.

Beyond its impressive facilities, the Dr. Phillips Center is committed to arts education and community engagement. It offers a variety of educational programs, workshops, and masterclasses aimed at nurturing local talent and fostering a love for the arts within the community. The center's commitment to accessibility and inclusion is evident in its diverse programming, which features performances from a wide range of genres and cultural traditions.

The Dr. Phillips Center for the Performing Arts not only enriches Orlando's cultural landscape but also serves as a gathering place for the community, providing a venue where people can come together to experience the transformative power of the arts. Whether attending a Broadway blockbuster, a symphony concert, or a local theater production, visitors to the Dr. Phillips Center are guaranteed an unforgettable experience.

Bob Carr Theater

The Bob Carr Theater, located in downtown Orlando, is a historic and iconic venue that has been a central part of the city's cultural scene for decades. Originally opened in 1927 as the Orlando Municipal Auditorium, the theater was renamed in honor of Bob Carr, a former Orlando mayor who was instrumental in its development as a premier performing arts venue. With a seating capacity of over 2,400, the Bob Carr Theater has hosted a wide range of events, from Broadway productions and classical music concerts to lectures and community gatherings.

The theater is known for its grand, traditional design, featuring a spacious proscenium stage, elegant decor, and excellent acoustics, making it an ideal venue for a variety of performances. It has served as the home for the Orlando Philharmonic Orchestra, Orlando Ballet, and the Florida Symphony Youth Orchestra, among others, contributing significantly to the city's cultural fabric.

In recent years, the theater has undergone renovations to modernize its facilities while preserving its historic charm. These upgrades have enhanced the audience experience, ensuring that the Bob Carr Theater remains a beloved and functional space for the performing arts in Orlando.

The Bob Carr Theater's central location also makes it a convenient and popular destination for both locals and tourists. Its role as a venue for diverse performances and events continues to make it a cornerstone of Orlando's arts community, offering audiences the opportunity to experience high-quality entertainment in a classic, storied setting.

Orlando Repertory Theatre

The Orlando Repertory Theatre, affectionately known as "The REP," is a unique and dynamic theater dedicated to producing high-quality performances for young audiences and their families. Located in Loch Haven Park, The REP is a key player in Orlando's cultural landscape, offering a diverse range of productions that inspire, educate, and entertain.

The REP was established with the mission of creating exceptional theater experiences that engage and resonate with children, fostering a love for the arts at an early age. The theater's productions often include adaptations of beloved children's books, fairy tales, and original works that are both entertaining and thought-provoking. The REP's creative approach to storytelling, combined with its professional production values, ensures that each performance is a memorable experience for audiences of all ages.

In addition to its mainstage productions, The REP is deeply committed to education and outreach. The theater offers a variety of programs, including acting classes, summer camps, and workshops designed to nurture young talent and provide hands-on learning opportunities in the performing arts. These programs are tailored to different age groups and skill levels, ensuring that all children have the opportunity to explore their creativity in a supportive environment.

The Orlando Repertory Theatre also collaborates with local schools and community organizations to bring theater to a wider audience, making the arts accessible to all children in the Orlando area. The REP's commitment to inclusivity and education has made it a beloved institution for families, educators, and young theater enthusiasts.

Through its engaging productions and educational initiatives, The Orlando Repertory Theatre plays a vital role in enriching the cultural life of Central Florida. It provides a welcoming space where the magic of theater can be experienced and cherished by the next generation.

Mad Cow Theatre

Mad Cow Theatre, located in the heart of downtown Orlando, is a prominent player in the city's vibrant performing arts scene, known for its commitment to producing high-quality, thought-provoking theater. Founded in 1997, Mad Cow Theatre has established itself as a hub for both classic and contemporary plays, offering a diverse range of performances that challenge, inspire, and entertain.

The theater is characterized by its intimate setting, which allows for a close connection between the audience and the performers. With a seating capacity of around 160, the venue creates an engaging and immersive experience, making each performance feel personal and impactful. Mad Cow Theatre's programming includes a mix of well-known classics, modern dramas, comedies, and musicals, as well as works by emerging playwrights. This eclectic selection ensures that there is something for everyone, from avid theatergoers to those new to live performance.

Mad Cow Theatre is also committed to fostering local talent and providing a platform for both seasoned and emerging actors, directors, and playwrights. The theater's emphasis on artistic excellence and creative exploration has garnered it a loyal following and critical acclaim within the Orlando arts community.

In addition to its regular season productions, Mad Cow Theatre offers educational programs, including workshops, masterclasses, and internships, aimed at nurturing the next generation of theater artists. The theater also engages with the community through special events, talkbacks, and collaborations with other local arts organizations.

Mad Cow Theatre's dedication to artistic integrity and its role as a cultural cornerstone in downtown Orlando make it a must-visit destination for anyone interested in experiencing the power of live theater. Whether you're attending a classic play, a contemporary piece, or a new work by a local playwright, Mad Cow Theatre promises a compelling and memorable experience.

Enzian Theater

The Enzian Theater, located in Maitland, Florida, just north of Orlando, is a beloved independent cinema that offers a unique and eclectic movie-going experience. Established in 1985, the Enzian is known for its commitment to showcasing independent, foreign, and classic films, as well as hosting a variety of film-related events and festivals that celebrate the art of cinema.

What sets the Enzian Theater apart is its distinctive ambiance and setting. The theater is nestled in a lush, garden-like environment, complete with outdoor seating areas and a picturesque courtyard, creating a relaxed and inviting atmosphere. Inside, the Enzian features a single, large-screen auditorium with a cozy, cabaret-style seating arrangement. Patrons can enjoy food and drinks from the theater's full-service kitchen and bar, Eden Bar, while watching a film, adding to the overall experience.

Enzian's programming is diverse, catering to a wide range of cinematic tastes. In addition to regular screenings of independent and international films, the theater hosts a number of annual film festivals, including the Florida Film Festival, one of the most prestigious and well-attended film festivals in the Southeast. The theater also offers special series such as "Cult Classics" and "Midnight Movies," which draw cinephiles and casual moviegoers alike.

Beyond its role as a cinema, the Enzian is a community hub that fosters a love for film and supports local filmmakers through workshops, panels, and networking events. The theater's commitment to film education and its efforts to create a vibrant film culture in Central Florida have made it a cherished institution for both locals and visitors.

Whether you're a serious film buff or just looking for a unique night out, the Enzian Theater offers an unforgettable cinematic experience in a setting that celebrates the magic and artistry of film.

Kia Center

The Kia Center, located in downtown Orlando, is a state-of-the-art multi-purpose arena that serves as the epicenter for sports and entertainment in Central Florida. Opened in 2010, the Kia Center is home to the NBA's Orlando Magic and the ECHL's Orlando Solar Bears, making it a premier destination for sports fans. With a seating capacity of up to 20,000, the arena is designed to accommodate a wide range of events, including concerts, family shows, and large-scale conventions.

The Kia Center is renowned for its modern design and cutting-edge technology, offering an enhanced experience for all attendees. The arena features spacious concourses, a variety of food and beverage options, and numerous premium seating areas, including luxury suites and club seats that provide an upscale viewing experience. The state-of-the-art scoreboard and sound system ensure that every seat in the house offers a clear view and an immersive audio experience.

Beyond sports, the Kia Center hosts some of the biggest names in music, with concerts spanning all genres from pop and rock to hip-hop and country. The venue has welcomed world-class artists such as Paul McCartney, Beyoncé, and Elton John, making it a key stop for major tours. The arena also regularly hosts special events, including WWE wrestling, Cirque du Soleil, and other large-scale performances that draw crowds from across the region.

The Kia Center's central location in downtown Orlando makes it easily accessible, with ample parking and public transportation options available. Its role as a premier entertainment venue, combined with its modern amenities and diverse programming, makes the Kia Center a must-visit destination for anyone looking to experience top-tier sports and entertainment in Orlando.

House of Blues Orlando

House of Blues Orlando, located in the vibrant Disney Springs entertainment district, is a renowned live music venue that combines Southern-inspired cuisine with top-notch performances in an intimate, soulful setting. Part of the iconic House of Blues chain, this Orlando location is known for its eclectic lineup of live music, featuring everything from rock and blues to hip-hop and electronic dance music. With its cozy, yet lively atmosphere, the venue attracts both locals and tourists looking to enjoy great music and a memorable night out.

The House of Blues Orlando is designed to evoke the spirit of the Deep South, with its distinctive decor featuring folk art, blues memorabilia, and rustic accents that create a warm and inviting ambiance. The venue includes a main music hall, which can accommodate up to 2,000 guests, and offers both standing room and balcony seating, ensuring a close connection between performers and the audience. The superior acoustics and lighting add to the immersive concert experience, making it one of Orlando's top spots for live music.

In addition to live performances, House of Blues Orlando is home to the popular restaurant and bar, which serves a menu inspired by Southern cuisine, including dishes like jambalaya, gumbo, and pulled pork sandwiches. The venue also hosts the famous "Gospel Brunch" on Sundays, where guests can enjoy a delicious buffet while being treated to uplifting gospel music performances.

House of Blues Orlando is more than just a concert venue; it's a cultural experience that celebrates music, art, and Southern hospitality. Whether you're there to see a favorite band, discover new music, or simply enjoy the food and atmosphere, House of Blues Orlando offers a unique and vibrant setting that leaves a lasting impression on all who visit.

Orlando Shakespeare Theater

The Orlando Shakespeare Theater, often referred to as Orlando Shakes, is a cornerstone of Central Florida's cultural scene, dedicated to bringing the works of William Shakespeare and other classic and contemporary playwrights to life. Located in the Lowndes Shakespeare Center in Loch Haven Park, Orlando Shakes has been producing professional theater since 1989 and has earned a reputation for excellence in both its performances and community outreach.

Orlando Shakes is renowned for its high-quality productions that range from Shakespeare's timeless plays to modern dramas, comedies, and musicals. The theater's commitment to artistic integrity and innovation ensures that each performance is thoughtfully staged, whether it's a fresh take on a Shakespearean classic or a world premiere of a new work. The theater's intimate performance spaces allow for an engaging and immersive experience, where audiences can connect deeply with the story and the characters.

In addition to its regular season, Orlando Shakes hosts the annual Orlando Shakespeare Festival, which draws theater lovers from across the region. The festival features a diverse lineup of plays, workshops, and events that celebrate the Bard's legacy and the enduring power of live theater.

Orlando Shakes is also deeply committed to education and community engagement. The theater offers a wide range of educational programs, including acting classes, summer camps, and school matinees, designed to inspire a love of theater in young people. These programs are complemented by outreach initiatives that bring theater into schools and underserved communities, making the arts accessible to a broader audience.

Through its exceptional productions, educational programs, and dedication to fostering a vibrant arts community, the Orlando Shakespeare Theater plays a vital role in enriching the cultural landscape of Central Florida. It offers audiences the opportunity to experience the magic of live theater in a setting that honors the past while embracing the present and future of the performing arts.

Plaza Live Orlando

Plaza Live Orlando, located in the heart of Orlando's Milk District, is a historic and beloved venue that has been a fixture of the city's entertainment scene since it first opened as a movie theater in 1963. Over the years, the Plaza Live has evolved into a versatile performance space that hosts a wide range of events, including live concerts, comedy shows, theater productions, and community events, making it one of the most diverse and active venues in Central Florida.

With its retro charm and intimate atmosphere, Plaza Live Orlando provides a unique setting for live performances. The venue has a seating capacity of approximately 900, which allows for a more personal and engaging experience, whether you're attending a rock concert, an acoustic set, or a comedy show. The theater's excellent acoustics and sightlines ensure that every seat in the house offers a great view and sound, making it a favorite among both performers and audiences.

Plaza Live is known for its eclectic programming, featuring a mix of national touring acts, local talent, and a variety of genres, from indie rock and jazz to folk and classical music. The venue has hosted performances by iconic artists such as Elvis Costello, Joe Jackson, and Joan Baez, as well as up-and-coming acts, providing a platform for both established and emerging musicians.

In addition to music, Plaza Live Orlando is also home to theatrical productions, film screenings, and special events, making it a cultural hub that caters to a wide range of interests. The venue's commitment to community engagement is evident in its partnerships with local organizations and its support of Orlando's vibrant arts scene.

Plaza Live Orlando offers a distinctive and welcoming environment where audiences can enjoy high-quality performances in a setting that reflects the city's rich cultural heritage. Whether you're a music lover, theater enthusiast, or simply looking for a night out, Plaza Live provides an unforgettable entertainment experience in the heart of Orlando.

The Beacham

The Beacham, located in the heart of downtown Orlando, is a historic and iconic nightclub and concert venue that has been a staple of the city's nightlife and entertainment scene for over a century. Originally opened in 1921 as a vaudeville theater, The Beacham has undergone several transformations throughout its history, evolving from a cinema to a music venue, and finally into the vibrant nightclub and concert hall that it is today. Its rich history and dynamic atmosphere make The Beacham a must-visit destination for both locals and visitors looking to experience Orlando's energetic nightlife.

The Beacham is renowned for its eclectic lineup of live music, featuring performances by a diverse array of artists spanning genres such as hip-hop, electronic, rock, and pop. The venue has hosted both legendary acts like The Police, Kendrick Lamar, and Drake, as well as up-and-coming artists, making it a key stop on the tour circuit for national and international performers. The venue's spacious layout, state-of-the-art sound system, and vibrant lighting create an electrifying environment that enhances the concert experience, making every performance memorable.

In addition to live music, The Beacham is also a popular nightclub, known for its high-energy dance nights and themed events. The club's DJs spin a mix of the latest hits and classic tracks, drawing large crowds of partygoers who come to dance the night away. The venue's multiple bars and VIP areas add to the upscale yet accessible vibe, ensuring that there's something for everyone.

The Beacham's central location, historic charm, and reputation for hosting top-tier entertainment make it a cornerstone of downtown Orlando's nightlife. Whether you're there for a concert, a DJ set, or just to soak up the atmosphere, The Beacham offers an unforgettable experience in one of the city's most iconic venues.

SAK Comedy Lab

SAK Comedy Lab, located in downtown Orlando, is a beloved improv comedy theater that has been entertaining audiences with laughter and creativity for over three decades. Founded in 1991, SAK Comedy Lab is known for its high-energy, family-friendly shows that showcase the talents of Orlando's top improvisers. With its intimate setting, welcoming atmosphere, and emphasis on audience participation, SAK Comedy Lab has become a cornerstone of the city's arts and entertainment scene.

The theater specializes in short-form improv, where performers create spontaneous scenes and sketches based on suggestions from the audience. Each show is entirely unique, as the comedians rely on their quick wit and creativity to craft hilarious and unpredictable performances in real time. The interactive nature of the shows means that no two performances are ever the same, making each visit to SAK Comedy Lab a fresh and exciting experience.

SAK Comedy Lab offers a variety of shows throughout the week, catering to different tastes and age groups. Popular shows include the signature "Duel of Fools," a fast-paced competition where improvisers go head-to-head in a series of comedic challenges, and "Gorilla Theatre," where the performers take turns directing scenes, leading to unexpected and often outrageous outcomes. The theater also hosts special events and themed shows, adding to its diverse lineup of entertainment.

In addition to its performances, SAK Comedy Lab is dedicated to nurturing new talent through its improv training program. The theater offers classes and workshops for aspiring improvisers of all skill levels, providing an opportunity to learn the art of improv in a supportive and fun environment.

With its commitment to quality entertainment, community engagement, and the art of improv, SAK Comedy Lab is a must-visit destination for anyone looking to enjoy a night of laughter and spontaneity in Orlando. Whether you're a first-time visitor or a longtime fan, SAK Comedy Lab guarantees an evening of fun, creativity, and unforgettable comedy.

Historical Sites

Kennedy Space Center Visitor Complex

The Kennedy Space Center Visitor Complex, located on Florida's Space Coast near Cape Canaveral, is an iconic destination that offers visitors an immersive journey into the history and future of space exploration. As the gateway to NASA's launch operations since the 1960s, the Kennedy Space Center is a place where history was made, and today, it continues to inspire and educate millions of visitors each year.

The Visitor Complex provides a wide range of exhibits, attractions, and experiences that celebrate the achievements of the U.S. space program. One of the main highlights is the Space Shuttle Atlantis exhibit, where visitors can get up close to the actual Atlantis orbiter, which flew 33 missions into space. The exhibit offers interactive displays and simulators that give a sense of what it's like to launch into space, dock with the International Space Station, and re-enter Earth's atmosphere.

Another must-see is the Rocket Garden, which showcases historic rockets that played key roles in the Mercury, Gemini, and Apollo programs. Visitors can also experience the Apollo/Saturn V Center, where a fully restored Saturn V rocket, the largest ever flown, is displayed. This exhibit tells the story of the Apollo missions, including the historic Apollo 11 moon landing.

The Kennedy Space Center Visitor Complex also offers guided tours that take visitors behind the scenes to see launch pads, the Vehicle Assembly Building, and other facilities that are integral to space missions. Educational programs, astronaut encounters, and IMAX films further enhance the experience, making it a fascinating and educational outing for all ages.

Whether you're a space enthusiast, a history buff, or just looking for an inspiring experience, the Kennedy Space Center Visitor Complex offers an unforgettable exploration of humanity's journey beyond Earth's atmosphere.

Fort Christmas Historical Park

Fort Christmas Historical Park, located in Christmas, Florida, offers visitors a unique glimpse into the history of the region, particularly during the Seminole Wars of the 19th century. Established as a replica of the original Fort Christmas, which was built by U.S. Army soldiers on Christmas Day in 1837 during the Second Seminole War, the park serves as both a historical site and a community hub, celebrating the heritage and pioneer spirit of Central Florida.

The centerpiece of the park is the full-scale replica of Fort Christmas, complete with blockhouses, a stockade, and historical exhibits that provide insight into the lives of the soldiers who were stationed there. The fort's museum features artifacts, documents, and displays that explain the significance of the Seminole Wars, the challenges faced by the soldiers, and the interactions between the military and the local Seminole population.

In addition to the fort, the park is home to a collection of restored historical buildings that reflect pioneer life in the 19th and early 20th centuries. These include a schoolhouse, a sugar cane mill, a cracker house, and a variety of other structures that offer a window into the daily lives of Florida's early settlers. Each building is furnished with period-appropriate artifacts, creating an authentic and educational experience.

Fort Christmas Historical Park also hosts a variety of community events throughout the year, including the popular Cracker Christmas festival, which features historical reenactments, traditional crafts, and pioneer demonstrations. The park's picnic areas, playgrounds, and nature trails make it a great destination for families looking to enjoy a day outdoors while learning about Florida's rich history.

Fort Christmas Historical Park is a valuable cultural and educational resource that preserves and celebrates the pioneer heritage of Central Florida. Whether you're a history enthusiast or simply looking for a peaceful and informative outing, the park offers a meaningful connection to the past.

Casa Feliz Historic Home Museum

Casa Feliz Historic Home Museum, located in the charming city of Winter Park, Florida, is a beautifully restored Spanish farmhouse-style home that stands as a testament to the region's rich architectural and cultural history. Designed by acclaimed architect James Gamble Rogers II in 1933, Casa Feliz, which means "Happy House" in Spanish, is a stunning example of Andalusian-style architecture, featuring a distinctive red-tiled roof, white stucco walls, and arched doorways that exude old-world charm.

Originally built as the residence of noted industrialist Robert Bruce Barbour, Casa Feliz is now a museum that preserves the architectural beauty and historical significance of the home. The house was saved from demolition in 2001 and carefully relocated to its current location overlooking the Winter Park Golf Course, where it was restored to its former glory.

Visitors to Casa Feliz can explore the home's exquisite interior, which includes original architectural features such as hand-carved wooden beams, decorative tile work, and intricate ironwork. The museum offers guided tours that provide insights into the history of the house, the life of its original inhabitants, and the architectural legacy of James Gamble Rogers II. The lushly landscaped gardens surrounding the house further enhance the picturesque setting, offering a serene environment for reflection and photography.

Casa Feliz also serves as a popular venue for cultural events, concerts, art exhibitions, and weddings, making it a vibrant part of the Winter Park community. Its unique blend of historical significance, architectural beauty, and cultural activity makes Casa Feliz a must-visit destination for those interested in history, architecture, and the arts.

Whether you're an architecture enthusiast or simply looking to enjoy a peaceful stroll through a beautifully preserved historic home, Casa Feliz offers a glimpse into Winter Park's past and the timeless elegance of Spanish-style architecture.

Food and Dining

Orlando may be known for its theme parks, but the city's culinary scene offers a delightful array of iconic foods that are cherished by locals and visitors alike. From Cuban sandwiches to citrus-inspired dishes and key lime pie, these quintessential Orlando eats reflect the diverse cultural influences and vibrant flavors of the region.

Cuban Sandwiches

Orlando's Cuban sandwiches are a must-try, reflecting the city's rich Cuban heritage. These sandwiches are characterized by their pressed, crusty bread and flavorful fillings, including roast pork, ham, Swiss cheese, pickles, and mustard. The bread, often brushed with butter, is toasted to perfection, giving the sandwich its signature crunch.

History: Cuban sandwiches, or "Cubanos," are believed to have originated among Cuban immigrant communities in Florida, including those in Orlando. They have become a staple in local eateries, particularly in the neighborhoods with strong Cuban and Latino influences.

Where to Find the Best Cuban Sandwiches:

- **Black Bean Deli:** Known for its authentic Cuban dishes, Black Bean Deli serves up some of the best Cuban sandwiches in Orlando, with fresh ingredients and traditional preparation.
- **Café Tu Tu Tango:** This eclectic restaurant offers a creative twist on the classic Cuban sandwich, incorporating unique flavors and a vibrant atmosphere.
- **Zaza New Cuban Diner:** A popular spot for both locals and tourists, Zaza offers a traditional Cuban sandwich experience, along with other Cuban delicacies.

Citrus-Inspired Dishes

Florida is famous for its citrus fruits, and Orlando's culinary scene takes full advantage of this local bounty. Citrus-inspired dishes and drinks, featuring oranges, grapefruits, and lemons, are a highlight in many restaurants.

Popular Citrus Dishes:

- **Citrus Salads:** Often featuring segments of fresh oranges or grapefruits, these salads are a refreshing and healthy option, frequently paired with local seafood.
- **Citrus-Glazed Chicken or Fish:** A favorite in many Orlando restaurants, this dish combines the tangy sweetness of citrus with savory proteins.
- **Craft Cocktails:** Many local bars and restaurants offer craft cocktails made with fresh citrus juices, perfect for cooling down in the Florida heat.

Where to Enjoy Citrus-Inspired Cuisine:

- **The Boathouse:** Located in Disney Springs, The Boathouse offers a variety of citrus-infused dishes, including seafood and cocktails, all enjoyed with stunning waterfront views.
- **Cask & Larder:** This Southern-inspired restaurant features locally sourced ingredients, including citrus, in its seasonal dishes and craft beers.
- **4 Rivers Smokehouse:** Known for its barbecue, 4 Rivers also incorporates citrus flavors into its sauces and sides, providing a unique twist on traditional Southern fare.

Key Lime Pie

Key lime pie, with its tart and sweet flavor, is a quintessential Florida dessert that has a special place in Orlando's culinary offerings. Made from Key lime juice, sweetened condensed milk, and a graham cracker crust, this dessert is a refreshing treat, especially in the warm Florida climate.

History: Key lime pie is a classic Florida dessert, originating from the Florida Keys. It has become a beloved dish across the state, including in Orlando, where many restaurants put their unique spin on this iconic pie.

Where to Find the Best Key Lime Pie:

- **The Ravenous Pig:** This gastropub offers a modern take on Key lime pie, incorporating local ingredients and creative presentation.
- **The Cheesecake Factory:** While a national chain, The Cheesecake Factory's Key lime cheesecake offers a rich, creamy twist on the traditional pie, popular among locals and visitors.
- **Key Lime Pie Bakery:** Specializing in this iconic dessert, this bakery provides a classic and authentic Key lime pie experience, perfect for dessert lovers.

Each of these iconic foods—Cuban sandwiches, citrus-inspired dishes, and Key lime pie—offers a taste of Orlando's rich culinary landscape. Enjoying these dishes is not just about savoring great flavors; it's also about experiencing the cultural diversity and local traditions that make Orlando's food scene so unique and delightful.

Fine Dining

Orlando's dining scene is renowned for its diversity and innovation, offering a range of fine dining experiences that attract food enthusiasts from around the world. The city boasts several acclaimed restaurants, including those recognized by the prestigious Michelin Guide, as well as a variety of internationally inspired establishments and casual eateries.

Michelin-Recognized Restaurants

Orlando's fine dining landscape includes several Michelin-recognized restaurants, celebrated for their exceptional cuisine, meticulous attention to detail, and impeccable service.

- **Victoria & Albert's:** Located in Disney's Grand Floridian Resort & Spa, Victoria & Albert's is a AAA Five Diamond award-winning restaurant. Renowned for its exquisite multi-course tasting menus and elegant ambiance, this restaurant offers a refined dining experience that highlights the finest ingredients and culinary techniques.

- **Kadence:** A Michelin-starred sushi and sake bar located in the Audubon Park Garden District, Kadence offers an intimate omakase dining experience. With a focus on fresh, high-quality seafood and traditional Japanese techniques, Kadence has become a favorite for sushi aficionados.
- **Capa:** Situated atop the Four Seasons Resort Orlando at Walt Disney World Resort, Capa is a sophisticated steakhouse and tapas bar. Known for its prime cuts of meat, fresh seafood, and stunning rooftop views, Capa provides a luxurious dining experience with a Spanish flair.

Internationally Inspired Fine Dining

Orlando's international dining scene is vibrant and diverse, featuring restaurants that bring global flavors to the city.

- **Norman's:** Chef Norman Van Aken's flagship restaurant, Norman's, is a pioneer of New World cuisine, blending Latin, Caribbean, and Asian influences. Located at the Ritz-Carlton Orlando, Grande Lakes, the restaurant offers a unique culinary journey that reflects Florida's rich cultural tapestry.
- **Chatham's Place:** A fine dining institution in Orlando, Chatham's Place offers a menu that emphasizes fresh, local ingredients with a touch of European elegance. The restaurant is known for its intimate setting and personalized service, making it a favorite for special occasions.
- **Prato:** This Winter Park gem offers a contemporary take on Italian cuisine, with a menu that features handmade pastas, wood-fired pizzas, and a variety of seasonal dishes. Prato's stylish atmosphere and inventive menu make it a popular destination for both locals and visitors.

Casual Eateries

Orlando's casual dining scene is just as vibrant, offering a range of eateries that deliver delicious food in a relaxed setting.

These casual spots are beloved by locals for their inviting atmospheres and consistently great food.

- **Se7en Bites:** A bakery and cafe in the Milk District, Se7en Bites is famous for its Southern-inspired comfort food, including biscuits, pies, and their signature chicken pot pie. The cozy atmosphere and hearty dishes make it a popular brunch destination.
- **The Ravenous Pig:** An American gastropub in Winter Park, The Ravenous Pig offers a menu that showcases local ingredients and craft beers. Known for its inventive dishes and laid-back vibe, it's a great spot for both casual dining and special occasions.
- **Pom Pom's Teahouse & Sandwicheria:** Located in the Milk District, Pom Pom's is known for its creative sandwiches, teas, and desserts. The eclectic decor and unique flavor combinations make it a must-visit for foodies.

Trendy Cafes and Diners

Orlando also has a vibrant selection of trendy cafes and diners offering everything from classic American fare to innovative brunch dishes.

The Glass Knife: A stylish bakery and cafe in Winter Park, The Glass Knife is renowned for its beautiful pastries, cakes, and savory brunch items. The chic interior and delectable treats make it a popular spot for both locals and visitors.

East End Market: This neighborhood market and food hall in Audubon Park features a variety of vendors offering everything from gourmet cheese and fresh bread to craft coffee and artisanal ice cream. It's a great place to sample local flavors and discover new favorites.

The Coop: A Southern-inspired restaurant in Winter Park, The Coop offers a menu of comfort food classics, including fried chicken, mac and cheese, and pecan pie. The warm, welcoming atmosphere and generous portions make it a favorite for family dining.

Each of these fine dining and casual dining spots showcases the rich culinary diversity of Orlando, offering visitors and locals alike a taste of the city's vibrant food culture. Whether you're in the mood for a luxurious meal or a laid-back bite, Orlando's dining scene has something for everyone.

Street Food and Food Trucks

Orlando's street food and food truck scene is lively and diverse, offering a convenient and flavorful way to experience the city's culinary offerings. From classic street food to gourmet food trucks, these mobile eateries are an integral part of Orlando's food culture.

Classic Street Food

Orlando's classic street food vendors provide quick and delicious snacks that are perfect for enjoying on the go.

- **Soft Pretzels:** A popular snack in busy areas, soft pretzels in Orlando are often served warm and topped with a sprinkle of salt. These pretzels are a satisfying treat, perfect for a quick bite during a day out exploring the city.
- **Latin Street Food:** Reflecting Orlando's diverse population, Latin food trucks and street vendors offer delicious dishes like empanadas, arepas, and tamales. These vendors provide an authentic taste of Latin American cuisine and are popular among both locals and tourists.

Gourmet Food Trucks

Orlando's food truck scene has seen significant growth, with gourmet trucks offering inventive and high-quality dishes from a variety of cuisines.

- **Korean BBQ Taco Box:** This food truck blends Korean flavors with classic street food, serving dishes like bulgogi tacos and kimchi fries. The unique fusion of flavors makes it a popular choice among food truck enthusiasts.
- **The Pastrami Project:** Specializing in traditional Jewish deli-style sandwiches, The Pastrami Project offers hearty sandwiches

filled with house-cured pastrami, corned beef, and other deli favorites. It's a great option for those seeking a taste of New York-style deli food in Orlando.

- **Twisted Plates:** Known for its creative comfort food, Twisted Plates serves up dishes like loaded mac and cheese and gourmet grilled cheese sandwiches. The truck's innovative menu attracts a diverse crowd, eager to try new and exciting flavors.

Pop-Up Markets

In addition to individual food trucks, Orlando hosts several pop-up markets and food truck gatherings where multiple vendors come together to offer a variety of street food options.

- **Tasty Takeover:** Held in the Milk District, Tasty Takeover is a weekly food truck event featuring a rotating selection of vendors. The event offers a wide range of cuisines, from BBQ and tacos to gourmet desserts.
- **Orlando Food Truck Bazaar:** This traveling food truck event brings together some of the best food trucks from around the area. It's a fantastic opportunity to sample a diverse array of dishes all in one place.

Ethnic Cuisine

Orlando's multicultural population is reflected in its vibrant ethnic food scene, offering a rich tapestry of flavors from around the world. Neighborhoods like Little Vietnam, Little India, and the various Latin American enclaves are known for their authentic and delicious cuisine.

Little Vietnam

Orlando's Little Vietnam district, located near Mills 50, is a culinary hotspot known for its authentic Vietnamese cuisine. This area offers a wide range of traditional dishes, from pho (Vietnamese noodle soup) to banh mi (Vietnamese sandwiches).

- **Pho 88:** A staple in the area, Pho 88 is renowned for its rich and flavorful pho, as well as other Vietnamese specialties like spring rolls and bun thit nuong (grilled pork with vermicelli noodles).
- **Vietnam Cuisine:** This restaurant offers a broad menu featuring Vietnamese favorites such as bun bo Hue (spicy beef noodle soup) and goi cuon (fresh spring rolls). The authentic flavors and cozy atmosphere make it a popular spot.

Little India

Located along the International Drive area, Little India is a vibrant community where visitors can enjoy authentic Indian cuisine.

- **Aashirwad Indian Cuisine:** Known for its modern interpretation of classic Indian dishes, Aashirwad offers a menu that includes traditional favorites like butter chicken and biryani, as well as innovative dishes that showcase the diversity of Indian cuisine.
- **Woodlands:** A vegetarian Indian restaurant, Woodlands specializes in South Indian cuisine, offering dishes like dosas (savory crepes) and idlis (steamed rice cakes). It's a favorite among vegetarians and lovers of Indian food.

Latin American Enclaves

Orlando's Latin American communities bring a rich culinary diversity to the city, with neighborhoods and restaurants offering flavors from Cuba, Puerto Rico, Mexico, and beyond.

- **Zaza New Cuban Diner:** A local favorite, Zaza offers classic Cuban dishes like ropa vieja (shredded beef) and lechon asado (roast pork), served with traditional sides like black beans and plantains.
- **Taco China:** Combining Chinese and Mexican influences, Taco China offers a unique fusion of flavors with dishes like Kung Pao tacos and teriyaki burritos. This innovative food spot reflects Orlando's diverse culinary scene.
- **Lechonera Latina:** Specializing in Puerto Rican cuisine, Lechonera Latina is known for its lechon (roast pork) and mofongo (mashed plantains with garlic and pork cracklings). The

restaurant provides an authentic taste of Puerto Rican culture and food.

Orlando's street food, food trucks, and ethnic cuisine offer a delicious and diverse culinary journey. Whether you're grabbing a quick bite from a food truck, enjoying traditional dishes in one of the city's ethnic neighborhoods, or exploring gourmet offerings, Orlando's food scene has something to satisfy every palate.

Food Markets

Orlando boasts a vibrant food scene that reflects its diverse cultural landscape. The city's food markets are excellent destinations for food lovers seeking a wide array of flavors and culinary delights. Among these, East End Market and the Orlando Farmers Market stand out as must-visit spots for locals and visitors alike.

East End Market

Located in the Audubon Park Garden District, East End Market is one of Orlando's premier indoor food markets. This community-focused market is housed in a charming two-story building, featuring a mix of artisanal food vendors, local artisans, and creative entrepreneurs. The market's rustic and inviting atmosphere, with wooden beams and cozy seating areas, makes it a popular gathering spot.

East End Market offers a diverse selection of culinary delights, catering to a wide range of tastes and preferences. Visitors can find everything from freshly baked bread and gourmet coffee to organic produce and handcrafted chocolates. Popular vendors include Gideon's Bakehouse, known for its indulgent cookies, and La Femme du Fromage, which offers a curated selection of cheeses and charcuterie.

In addition to its food stalls, East End Market features several sit-down eateries where visitors can enjoy a full meal. Domu, an acclaimed ramen shop, serves flavorful bowls of ramen and unique small plates, while Farm & Haus offers a menu focused on healthy and locally-sourced dishes. The market also houses retail shops selling unique gifts, kitchenware, and

75

specialty foods, making it a one-stop destination for both culinary delights and shopping.

Orlando Farmers Market

The Orlando Farmers Market is a beloved open-air market held every Sunday at Lake Eola Park in downtown Orlando. This market is a staple for both locals and tourists, offering a lively atmosphere and a wide variety of fresh produce, prepared foods, and artisanal products.

Operating year-round, the Orlando Farmers Market features dozens of local vendors offering everything from seasonal fruits and vegetables to homemade jams and baked goods. It's an excellent place to explore the flavors of Central Florida, with vendors like Wild Ocean Seafood Market providing fresh seafood straight from Florida's waters, and local farmers offering organic and sustainably grown produce.

One of the highlights of the Orlando Farmers Market is its diverse selection of international foods. Visitors can enjoy a variety of cuisines, including Latin American dishes, Mediterranean specialties, and Asian-inspired snacks. Food trucks and stalls offer a range of options, from empanadas and arepas to fresh sushi and gourmet crepes.

The market's scenic location by Lake Eola adds to its appeal, making it a perfect spot for a leisurely Sunday outing. Visitors can stroll through the market, enjoy live music, and even participate in yoga sessions held in the park. The Orlando Farmers Market not only provides a platform for local farmers and artisans but also fosters a sense of community and supports sustainable practices.

Both East End Market and the Orlando Farmers Market offer unique and memorable culinary experiences, showcasing the best of Orlando's vibrant food scene. Whether you're exploring the eclectic offerings at East End or enjoying the fresh and local flavors at the Farmers Market, these food markets are essential destinations for any food enthusiast visiting the city.

Made in United States
Orlando, FL
06 April 2025